Deo Gratias

Deo Gratias

Parish Heritage Cookbook
Written & Edited by
Anthony J. Rotolo, Ph.D.
with
The Marian Guild

Foreword by
Father Paul Angelicchio

St. John the Baptist &Transfiguration of
Our Lord Catholic Church of Rome, New York

2022

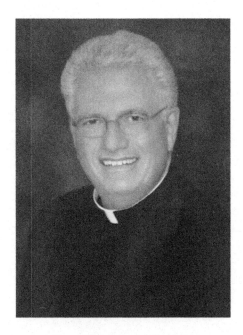

Rev. Paul Angelicchio
Pastor

In 1906, a small, determined group of Italian Immigrants began what we call St. John the Baptist Church. Over 100 years later, along with Transfiguration Parish, we celebrate the past and look forward to our future.

This cookbook is dedicated to the loyal members, past and present, of our Parish. A special thank you to the Marian Guild: it is through their effort and dedication that this cookbook is a reality. A special thank you to Anthony Rotolo, for his work in bringing everything together to make this book so special and a treasure for us to enjoy.

There is a bond among those who break bread together, a custom established by our Lord at the Last Super.

We hope that this collection of recipes from the past and present parishioners will benefit those who use them.

A special thank you to each one who took the time to share their favorite recipes that made this book possible. I can't wait to try each of them.

May the Lord Bless you and keep you and your families.

AUTHOR'S DEDICATIONS

This book is dedicated to my grandmother, Marie Rotolo, who served God through St. John the Baptist Church all her life. As president of the Marian Guild, she worked on many of the original parish cookbooks. I was inspired to create this special edition in her memory.

Me with my grandmother Marie Rotolo (right) and Aunt Angela "Angie" DiMeo

I also dedicate this book to Mary Katherine Swerediuk and Deborah DeCosty. As leaders of the St. John's Catholic Youth Organization, MaryK and Debbi created meaningful and fun opportunities to be involved in parish life; and some of my fondest childhood memories were spent with them. Both were called home to be with God sooner than we expected, and they are remembered always for their kindness, devotion, and service.

ACKNOWLEDGEMENTS

I wish to acknowledge those who made this project possible. First, I would like to thank my mother, MaryAnn Rotolo, who served as chair of the Marian Guild cookbook committee. I have relied on her historical knowledge of East Rome and her culinary expertise throughout this process. Truly, this book would not have been created without her leadership and wisdom; and, though she did not wish to be credited for it, she was indeed my co-author and co-editor.

In addition, I want to recognize the contributions of Patti Martinelli, Elizabeth Voci, Crystal D'Ambrosi, Sharon Puma, and Theresa Holmes. I enjoyed our productive and always entertaining meetings. Special thanks to Liz and Patti for a fantastic job leading the fundraising efforts.

On behalf of St. John's and Transfiguration Parish, I wish to thank the sponsors who generously supported this project. Please say a prayer for the loved ones who are memorialized on the sponsor page, and kindly support the local businesses listed there and in ads throughout.

I am also greatful for the help of T.K. Millo & Co. who handled the page design and layout for this book. Tennille and her team worked tirelessly to organize and assemble this volume for print, and the beautiful result reflects the expertise and professionalism they brought to this project.

And finally, my sincere thanks to Fr. Paul Angelicchio and the Marian Guild for the opportunity to work on this project, as well as all parishioners of St. John the Baptist and Transfiguration for your participation and encouragement. I have learned so much about our parish heritage from each of you, and I am honored to share your stories in this book.

— Anthony J. Rotolo, Ph.D.

St. John the Baptist & Transfiguration of Our Lord Church
would like to thank the following for their generous support of this book project.

In Memoriam

Marie & Percy Angelicchio

Dominick, Salmina, & Donna Mungari

Thank You to Our Local Sponsors

Ace Hardware of Rome

Bottini Funeral Home

Country Kitchen Restaurant

Ferlo's Bakery

Galliano Club of Rome, NY

Nicholas J. Bush Funeral Home

Nunn & Harper Funeral Home

Panasci Excavating

Puma Accounting, Inc.

Rocco Gualtieri's Italian Market

Rome Income Tax Service & Rizzo's Market

Steve Sislo, ChCF

Spresso's Coffee Cookies & Cakes, Inc.

Varano's Super Jump

TABLE OF CONTENTS

INTRODUCTION 15

OUR PARISH HERITAGE 19

THE SAINTS IN OUR LIVES 28

VISITING THE PARISH VISITORS 40

PRAYING THE HOLY ROSARY 44

APPETIZERS 49

BEVERAGES 54

BREADS, MUFFINS & ROLLS

Bread 57

Muffins 62

Rolls 63

SOUPS & SALADS

Salads 70

Soups 65

ENTREES

Beef 74

Casserole 79

Chicken 87

Fish 93

Macaroni 102

Pork 110

Stew 111

Veal 112

PIZZA & SAUSAGE BREAD 116

SIDES 120

SAUCES 125

PICKLES & RELISHES

Pickles 128

Pickled Vegetables 130

Relish 131

DESSERTS

Cake 133

Candy 158

Cookies 160

Granola 184

Pies & Crisps 185

Pastries 195

Pudding 202

Introduction
Anthony J. Rotolo, Ph.D.

> *On the third day there was a wedding in Cana in Galilee, and the mother of Jesus was there. Jesus and his disciples were also invited to the wedding. When the wine ran short, the mother of Jesus said to him, "They have no wine." [And] Jesus said to her, "Woman, how does your concern affect me? My hour has not yet come." His mother said to the servers, "Do whatever he tells you."*
>
> — Gospel of John (2:1-5), New American Bible

The Gospel story of the Wedding at Cana has always captured my imagination. It tells of the first time that Jesus Christ gave a public sign of His divinity by transforming water into wine. This was a pivotal moment in His life because Jesus knew that word of His miraculous deed would quickly spread. He and His disciples would soon attract a crowd, as well as danger from those opposed to His teaching. It is clear, then, why St. John chose to include this story in his Gospel: it marks the beginning of Jesus' public ministry and sets in motion the events leading to His passion, death, and resurrection. Looking closely at this story, however, there is still more to discover about the Wedding at Cana.

There are precious few moments in scripture that provide a look at Jesus' life prior to His ministry. The Gospel authors understandably focused on the events most important to the story of salvation; but the Wedding at Cana is one story where the two aspects of Christ's nature—human and divine—overlap in the narrative. Here we see Jesus at a wedding feast with his family and friends. If we imagine the scene, it looks much like a modern wedding: there is music and dancing, lively conversations, and plenty of food and drink for the guests. It is easy to imagine Jesus enjoying Himself, just as we would on such a happy occasion.

Whenever we plan a large event, there is always a chance that something will go wrong. In this case, the family did not order enough wine to accommodate the guests, and the supply had run out in the middle of the party. This was an embarrassing situation for the parents of the bride, just as it would be today. Mary, mother of Jesus, noticed the crisis unfolding; and, out of compassion for the family, she turned to her Son for help. Again, if we imagine the scene, we can picture how Mary might have tapped Jesus on the shoulder and whispered quietly, "They have no wine." Every son surely recognizes that this was both a statement and a request. We all know that special way mothers have of gently nudging us to help out when we would rather not get involved. Every son can therefore relate to our Lord when He asks His mother, "How does your concern affect me?"

This passage fascinated me when we read it in high school. Understanding the larger implications of the situation, it made sense that Jesus was hesitant to do what Mary asked: His "hour," or the time of His public ministry, had not yet come. What surprised me was how He replied to His mother, or rather how I interpreted the response. At Rome Catholic High, we used the older Douay-Rheims translation which reads, "Woman, what is that to me and to thee?" I took this statement to mean that Jesus did not want to be bothered by His mother's request. This was something that I, as a teenager, could certainly understand. Not fully grasping the context of His words, I reasoned (with teenage logic) that if Jesus had addressed His mother in this way, then it must be appropriate for me to do the same.

Later that week, I was watching television as my mom was busy doing work around the house. She popped her head into the living room and reminded me, "The trash needs to go out tonight." I quickly replied, "Woman, what is that to me?" Needless to say, that answer was not well received. To my surprise, my mother was not at all impressed that I was quoting scripture. "You better read it again!" she told me. "You missed the point!"

With further study, and more maturity, I came to understand that our Lord was not being dismissive toward His mother. First, and perhaps most important for my continued survival into adulthood, I learned that "Woman" was not considered a disrespectful form of address in Jesus' time, but that had apparently changed by the 20th Century. I also learned that the phrase, "what is that to me and you," was a common Hebrew saying that, in this case, meant something closer to "how am I involved?" or "why are you telling me this?"

With this knowledge, we can better imagine how the tone of the exchange between Jesus and Mary was likely more playful than confrontational. As sons (and daughters), we often lovingly joke with our mothers, feigning disinterest or ignorance before acquiescing to a well-meaning request. Jesus, pure of heart and free of sin, was no doubt doing the same. We can even imagine Him holding back a smile as He asks, "What does that have to do with me?" All the while, our Lord knew exactly what His mother was asking and that He would not refuse her. It seems that Mary knew as well, as she did not attempt to convince her Son any further. She simply turned to the servers and said, "Do whatever he tells you." These are Mary's last recorded words in the Holy Bible, and they were surely said with a smile.

Contemplating the Wedding at Cana story in this way helped me to understand my role as a son in adulthood, and to fully appreciate the relationship I have with my own mother. Though Jesus Christ was a perfect son, I most certainly am not; and, while my mother's heart is full of love for God and her family, neither is she immaculate as was our Lady. Jesus and Mary are, however, the models that all Catholics aspire to imitate; and I found an important takeaway in this story: if Christ honored His mother's request—knowing, as she did, the sacrifice it would require of Him—then I can surely do the same when my mother asks something far less of me.

I began this introduction with a discussion of the Wedding at Cana because, had I not learned from the example of Jesus in that story, the book you are holding would not exist. Though I have served as its author and editor, this book was my mother's idea. I can recall the day she came home from a Marian Guild meeting where she had proposed re-publishing the popular parish cookbooks of the last century. The idea was well received, and her fellow Guild members had appointed her chair of a cookbook committee. It was then that she told me a rather important detail: "I don't know how to publish a book." Of course, I already knew that; so, I just smiled and said, "What does that have to do with me?"

I am not a cook. I can boil macaroni, but unless I have my mother's sauce in the freezer, I have to open a jar—or just eat it with butter. What I lack in culinary skills, I hope I make up in my knowledge of research and writing. I am, after all, a psychologist trained to study people's stories; and, as I listened to my mother talk about the Marian Guild cookbooks of yesteryear, that is what stood out to me—stories. More than a collection of classic family recipes, the larger significance of the old cookbooks was the memories and traditions they represented. That was the reason they were still used and shared around Rome (and, as I would soon find out, far beyond). With so few copies remaining, it wasn't just the recipes we needed to preserve, but the stories of the people who made them. It was then that the project took shape, and we set out to create a book that could be shared with our children and grandchildren, just as those original cookbooks had been.

Though this book was a labor of love, it was not easy work. Together, my mother and I examined every St. John's cookbook produced by the Marian Guild, from the ever popular *What's Cookin' in Rome* of 1977 to the last edition printed in 2000. Then, thanks to the help of our committee members, and an old box of my late grandmother's belongings, we gathered crumbling copies of even older books created by the Ave Maria Sodality—the parish women's group that predated the Marian Guild—going back to the 1950s and 60s. Hundreds of pages had to be painstakingly scanned and converted into digital text so that we could work with them in a modern format. The process took many hours to complete, but we were thankful for the technology that prevented us from having to retype each recipe! Once the digital archive was complete, my mother spent many more hours reading through the pages, selecting the final list of recipes to appear in this book. This was where I relied on her culinary expertise, as I was not at

Our Parish Heritage: A Story of Faith, Family, and Food

The heritage of our perish is shaped by the cultures and traditions of the immigrants who settled in Rome, NY, around the turn of the last century. As the name of our city suggests, many of these families were from Italy. They arrived here via Ellis Island seeking new opportunities and better lives for their children. Some initially lived in the tenements of New York City, enduring extreme poverty and crime before leaving for more welcoming places upstate. Rome was a popular destination with a growing Italian American community and plentiful work available in its factories and mills. Others, like my paternal great grandparents, were attracted to Rome's farmland for its fertile soil—known as "muck"—that was ideal for raising bountiful crops of vegetables.

Arriving by the hundreds, and then by the thousands, the Italian immigrants made their homes in East Rome, along East Dominick Street, and in the South Rome neighborhoods extending from South James Street. They enriched the city with their culture and their labor; and soon it was brimming with immigrant-run businesses. From Ferlo's Bakery to Gualtieri's Market, the Savoy Restaurant to Mazzaferro's Meats, these and many other entrepreneurs made Rome synonymous with the finest Italian American foods in the region. The aroma of home cooking flowed from the kitchens of every home as well. Adapting old-world dishes to the local ingredients of their new home, as well as the scarcity of money and supplies during financial downturns, a distinct form of Italian American cuisine was being created. Beans and Greens, Pasta e Cici, Pasta e Fagioli, and other so-called "Depression dishes" were the family staples that became legendary favorites, as did the wine made from homegrown grapes or dandelions picked from the yard. Many of the recipes featured in this book were adapted from recipes passed down by the master cooks—the mothers and fathers—who first made them here in Rome.

Faith was another aspect of Italian culture passed down from the first immigrants who arrived. One of the many beautiful features of the Catholic Church is the tapestry of diverse traditions reflected in her parishes throughout the world. From Italy to Ireland, Germany and France, to the nations of Africa, Latin America and Asia, Catholics profess their faith in the one, holy, catholic (universal), and apostolic Church while retaining the unique qualities of their local cultures. For this reason, in America, which is a great melting pot of cultures, Catholic churches often reflect the ethnic heritage of their parishioners. As the Italian population of Rome grew, however, the city lacked a spiritual home for the traditions and devotions to which they had been accustomed in the old country (see *The Saints in Our Lives* by Gaetano Nasci in this volume for a detailed discussion of the customs of Italian American Catholics).

The Church of St. John the Baptist was incorporated in 1909 to serve the Italian American community of Rome. The small parish began in a building on the 300 block of East Dominic Street. By 1911, property was purchased on nearby River Street to accommodate the growing congregation. Father Vincenzo Giorgio, the first pastor, oversaw the completion of the River Street church in 1914. As the parish continued to grow rapidly, St. John's second pastor, Father Joseph Panesi, worked to expand the church and converted adjacent houses to add a rectory, classrooms for religious education, and a residence for the Parish Visitors of Mary Immaculate (see *Visiting the Parish Visitors* to learn more about the Sisters who served St. John's Parish for nearly 75 years). A small chapel at Mohawk and Third Streets was also converted to celebrate Sunday Mass.

By the late 1920s, St. John the Baptist Church was a vibrant parish, alive with Holy Masses, weddings, baptisms, and feast days around which spiritual and community life revolved for the Italian families of Rome. Now the parishioners longed for a place for their faithful departed to rest. In 1928, that dream was realized when, through the efforts of Joseph Bottini and other parish leaders, 20 acres of land were acquired along the north side of East Dominick Street. Presiding over the consecration of St. John the Baptist Cemetery, Fr. Panasci, speaking to the crowd in Italian, announced that the last object of their hope and aspiration had been realized. He noted the magnitude of the accomplishment as the first Italian

St. John the Baptist parishioners on the steps of the River Street church (c. 1925)

community in New York State to have a cemetery. "You shall pass on," he said, "but the memory of your efforts in the cemetery will live for many years to come."

St. John the Baptist moved to its present location on East Dominick Street in 1954. Under the direction of our third pastor, Father (later Monsignor) Victor Ciciarelli, the parish purchased the former site of the Rome Brass and Copper Company where a new church would be constructed. To raise funds for the building project, Fr. Ciciarelli organized the first St. John's Festival which was held on the site in 1949. These festivals would soon become a yearly tradition featuring amusement rides, games, raffles—and, of course, food. A highlight of summer for all Romans was to attend the St. John's Festival and enjoy some pizza fritta or a sausage and peppers sandwich. In its early years, two festivals were held in a year, raising $250,000 to fund the new church.

FIRST ST. JOHN'S CHURCH

Ferlo Block

E. Dominick St.

1911 — 1914

————

St. John the Baptist — River Street

1914 — 1954

Church Completes Plans For Three-Day Festival

Lacking $20,000 of its $250,000 building fund goal, St. John the Baptist Church will hold a three-day festival next month in the hope of raising the amount needed.

With Peter Coccia as chairman, the festival will be held on church-owned property on E. Dominick St., between Bouck St. and the Mohawk River Bridge.

The festival, slated Aug. 15, 16 and 17, will be sponsored by the Building Fund Committee which hopes to raise the additional funds necessary for construction this year of a new church on the festival site.

Final plans for the proposed new church have been approved by the Bishop's Building Commission, headed by the Rt. Rev. Msgr. David C. Gildey, secretary.

Bids for contracts will be received until 11 a.m. Aug. 19 at the rectory of St. John the Baptist Church and will be opened at 2 p.m. that day in the chancery office in Syracuse.

Committee Meets

Mr. Coccia was appointed festival chairman at the meeting of the Building Fund Committee which named the Rev. Victor F. Ciciarelli, pastor, and the Rev. William J. Lynch, assistant pastor, as honorary chairmen.

Attending the meeting were Chairman Anthony La Gatta, Peter and Sisto T. Coccia, Frank Coluccio, Louis Comis, James D. Ferrare Sr., Dominick Giambona, G. Edward La Gatta, Anthony J. Mariani, Dominick J. Parry, Joseph J. Ferlo and Joseph Rainone of the committee.

Father Ciciarelli expressed his appreciation to committee members for their work to date and urged them to do their utmost to raise the additional $20,000.

Peter Coccia

aug - 1952

UTICA, N. Y., TUESDAY MORNING, OCTOBER 28, 1952   PAGE NINE

BLASTING NECESSARY FOR CHURCH PROJECT—Excavation work for foundation of new St. John the Baptist Church on E. Dominick St. has been temporarily slowed by large underground sections of brick and concrete that were once part of old brass mill. Small charges of dynamite were used yesterday to break up pieces for removal by power shovels.

TO MAKE WAY FOR NEW CHURCH—The Rev. Victor F. Ciciarelli, pastor of St. John the Baptist Church, wields the sledge hammer to start demolition of the old Revere Copper Mill on E. Dominick St. A new $250,000 church is to be constructed on the site. Looking on is G. Edward La Gatta, chairman of a campaign, launched today, to raise the needed $75,000 for the church. The Building Fund Committee has $175,000 in cash. (Sentinel Photo)

Sodality Donates Total Of $5,500 to Church

With a check for $1,000, the Mother of Christ Sodality of St. John the Baptist Church last night raised their total contribution to the church building fund to $5,500.

The largest amount donated to the fund by any church organization, it represents the proceeds from suppers, socials and card parties sponsored by the 25 active members of the sodality.

GROUND-BREAKING — The Rev. Victor F. Ciciarelli, pastor of St. John the Baptist Church, digs the first shovelful of earth for the new church to be erected on E. Dominick St. The Rev. Leonard M. Barry is at right. Pa. ally shown behind Father Ciciarelli is Anthony La Gatta, chairman of the Building Fund Committee, while in the background at left is Joseph J. Ferlo. (Sentinel Photo)

St. John the Baptist Parishioners Reach $250,000 Building Fund Goal

HITS $250,000 TOP — St. John the Baptist Church has reached its $250,000 goal to construct a new edifice on E. Dominick St. Dominick Giambona, standing right with the Rev. Victor F. Ciciarelli, pastor, points to total on the campaign thermometer located at the proposed site. Left to right are Anthony J. Mariani, Fred P. Sestito, James Pettinelli, and Giambona, all prominent workers in the fund drive, and Father Ciciarelli. (Sentinel Photo)

The parishioners of St. John the Baptist Church have reached their $250,000 goal for construction of a new church on E. Dominick St., between Bouck and the Mohawk River Bridge, the Rev. Victor F. Ciciarelli, pastor, said today.

Construction is expected to begin by mid-October. Father Ciciarelli said specifications will be in the hands of general contractors this week-end and sealed bids should be ready for opening by the end of September.

"Work will start shortly after the general construction contract is let." Father Ciciarelli said.

Father Ciciarelli said $13,000 of the final $15,000 needed to top the goal was raised through the parish festival covering two week-ends. Another $2,000 was raised from cash donations obtained by the church's building fund committee, chairmaned by Anthony J. LaGatta.

Started in 1945

The drive, started in 1945, reached its final phase in March with $75,000 still to be raised. G. Edward LaGatta, local attorney, headed the summer campaign to raise this vitally-needed money.

"The committee will not be idle now that the goal has been reached," Father Ciciarelli emphasized. "It will try to take in as much more money as possible, as rising construction costs make this necessary."

Bids for the general contract work were opened Aug. 19, but no final decision was made because of an insufficient number of bids received.

To Receive New Bids

Father Ciciarelli said contract drawings and specifications have been mailed ot contractors in Rome and elsewhere and new bids will be received late in September.

The present church, located on River St., has long been considered inadequate for the rapidly-growing congregation, estimated between 8,000 and 10,000 persons of Italian birth and extraction.

The new edifice, to be constructed on property formerly occupied by the Brass Mill of Revere's Rome Division, will seat 744 in addition to a choir of 64. The basement will have social quarters accommodating more than 300 persons.

Today, St. John the Baptist & Transfiguration of Our Lord is home to parishioners reflecting a multitude of cultural backgrounds. Prominent among these are the Polish American roots of families whose forebearers immigrated to Rome around the same time as the Italians. Together, we share a story of hard work and perseverance, building new lives in a new world, and contributing greatly to the strength and prosperity of our city.

Many Polish Immigrants who arrived in America during the early 20th Century sought to escape political and military conflict in their homeland. Then divided under Russian, Prussian, and Austrian rule, the Polish people faced harsh living conditions and religious persecution for their Catholic faith. In addition, Polish men had been forced to serve in the Austrian Army during World War I. The war brought significant casualties and economic hardship; and, after Poland won its independence in 1920, the difficult living conditions remained. This led to the largest wave of Polish immigration to the United States. An additional wave came after World War II when millions of Polish people had lost their lives and homes, and the country found itself under communist rule. Facing persecution of Catholics by the atheistic Soviet Union, Polish immigrants again sought freedom in the United States.

Many Polish families settled in South Rome, alongside their Italian neighbors; and the two cultures found a strong bond together. Though they spoke different languages and faced different challenges on their journeys here, the two groups shared familiar traditions around family and faith. Fast friendships emerged between them, as well as many happy marriages celebrated at St. John's. Initially, the Polish American community of Rome did not have a spiritual center of their own. Attending Mass in private homes and in a social hall on South James Street, they longed for a church that reflected the traditions they had left behind in Poland. By 1909, property on the corner of Henry and South George Streets was purchased as the site of a new church—a wooden structure with seating for about 400 people.

Transfiguration of Our Lord Catholic Church was dedicated in 1920 after Father John Tarlowski purchased a nearby church on Ridge Street to accommodate the growing parish. Originally constructed in 1871 by Rome's German Catholic community, it was expanded in 1960, and a marble altar containing the sacred relics of Holy Martyrs St. Vincent and St. Felicitas was consecrated by Father Holocinski. The sanctuary was renovated again in the early 1970s, under Father Matthew Luczycki, and a new altar containing relics of St. Ignatius and St. Catherine Laboure was consecrated. In 2011, Bishop Robert Cunningham appointed Father Paul Angelicchio pastor of both Transfiguration and St. John the Baptist, merging the two churches into a single parish. Holy Mass now takes place at St. John's on Dominick Street, while Transfiguration on Ridge Street has been designated an oratory. There, parishioners take part in perpetual adoration of the Most Holy Sacrament.

The integration of Transfiguration and St. John the Baptist has enriched the spiritual life of our parish family. In addition to Eucharistic Adoration, Novena to the Blessed Mother, and other traditions, the heritage of our Transfiguration parishioners brings a special devotion to the Polish Saints who so deeply inspired Catholics around the world in the last century. These include St. Pope John Paul II and St. Maximillian Kolbie, martyr of Auschwitz, who are memorialized in a hand-carved wooden mural inside Transfiguration. A portrait of Christ depicting the vision of St. Faustina Kowalska now hangs above the entrance to the sanctuary at St. Johns, reminding all parishioners to make acts of mercy as Our Lord requested.

**1948 Marian Guild · 1st Fund Raiser for
St. John's New Church**

Front Row Seated: Mary DeMare, Phil Ferrare, Rev. Joseph Marangola, Mary Parry (Pres.), Lena Messineo, Anne DeMare. Standing L to R: Adeline Barone, Connie Guido, Anne Sega, Mary Mondromica, Mary Chicaferro, Mrs. Pinti, Flora Panieci, Jennie Pinti, Jean Colangelo, Pauline Bush, Rose Lombino, Ann Fiorenza, Barbara Detota. Top Row L to R: Sara Messinea, Rose Mistretta, Dolores Busciglio, Mary S. Bomoretto, Naz. Rohorcsak, Unknown, Shirley Sbarglia, Nina Daniello, Phil Kern.

We Break Bread Together

The Marian Guild has been serving our parish for over 60 years through spiritual and community initiatives. As a Catholic women's group, the Guild has a special devotion to the Blessed Virgin Mary, and members lead our congregation in praying the Holy Rosary each week before Mass (see our Guide to Praying the Rosary in this book). Since its founding, the Marian Guild has also taken a leading role in raising funds to support our parish. These activities have historically brought our community together for meals and celebrations. In 1948, the Guild held the first event to support construction of the new St. John the Baptist Church on East Dominick Street. The spaghetti dinner was sponsored by P&R Pasta of Auburn, NY—a favorite brand of many Italian American families in Rome.

Over the years, the Marian Guild has continued the tradition of hosting dinners and preparing classic favorites in our kitchen at the St. John's social hall. These include the popular Pasta e Cici dinner in celebration of St. Joseph's Day. Members also applied their cooking skills at the St. John's Festival by stretching and frying dough and serving other favorites at the busy food booths. The Guild's own Cake Booth was frequently a top draw at the Festival as guests lined up to take a spin on the wheel to win one of our delicious homemade cakes.

The Marian Guild's love of faith, family, and food are reflected throughout this book. For generations, we have come together around the table to enjoy the dishes and traditions collected in these pages. We hope the recipes and memories in this book delight you and fill your heart with love—the secret ingredient they all share. As we break bread together, let us give thanks to God—*Deo gratias*—for the many blessings we have received.

The Marian Guild (2022)

From left to right, seated Front Row: Cecilia "Ceil" Fiorini, Patricia Scaccia, Patricia Domenico, and Kathleen Loreto; Seated, 2nd row: Ersilia "Ceil" Ferris, Rosemarie Fragapane, Grace Pacicca, Mary Natalie; 3rd row: Angela Guglielmo, Lucille Hilts, Patricia Martinelli, Elizabeth Voci, Joanne Mitsou, Diana Sadlon, Cheryl Skogland, Crystal D'Ambrosi; 4th row: Delores Swinney, Dawn Beers, Delores Ferlo, Joan Hernandez, Laurie Guy, Marie Rossi, Maria Griffo, Sharon Puma, Father Paul Angelicchio

Marian Guild Officers
Kathleen Loreto, Facilitator
Crystal D'Ambrosi, Assistant Facilitator
Carlene Corigliano, Secretary
Marie Lynn Rossi, Treasurer
Patricia Martinelli, Bereavement Chair

Marian Guild Members
Doris Badolato, Dawn Beers, Grace Bottini, Deborah Brement, Mary Anne Casadei, Patricia Domenico, Mary Jane Doonan, Delores Ferlo, Ersilia "Ceil" Ferris, Cecilia "Ceil" Fiorini, Rosemarie Fragapane, Elizabeth "Betty" Gratch, Maria Griffo, Angela Guglielmo, Joan Hernandez, Lucille Hilts, Theresa Holmes, Joanne Mitsou, Sally Mungari, Mary Natalie, Kathleen O'Rourke; Grace Pacicca, Rose Parisi, Sharon Puma, Jeanette Redd, MaryAnn Rotolo, Diana Sadlon, Patricia Scaccia, Cheryl "Sherry" Skogland, Delores "Dee" Swinney, Marguerite "Margo" Taylor, Elizabeth Voci

The Saints in Our Lives

·····························

Customs and Legends Surrounding the Italian Immigrants' Old-World Patrons

by Gaetano Nasci

Editor's note: The following essay was written in 1994 by Gaetano Nasci and first published in the book, Italian American Heritage, edited by Nicholas D'Argenio and Carmen Malagisi. These men have since passed on, though their many contributions to St. John the Baptist Church are remembered fondly in our parish. This article reflects not only the depth of historical and cultural knowledge they possessed, but also the love they had for their Church and the Catholic faith. The original work is presented here, with minor editing, and is dedicated to their memory.

With his vivid descriptions of the River Street church and practices of venerating the Saints, Nasci brings to life pious traditions that were once commonplace in our parish and throughout the United States. It was the immigrants from Italy, Ireland, Poland, Germany, and other European countries that brought the Catholic faith to the New World; and theirs was a faith alive with ritual and reverence in which the Saints played a central role. Their Mass followed the same Latin Rite that inspired their patron saints to holiness; their churches were filled with the fragrance of incense and the sounds of Gregorian chant; and their social activities revolved around the Church calendar of holy days and religious festivals. The Catholic faith, then, was an essential part of their identities. Through the ancient practices of their ancestors, they connected their new lives in America with the world they left behind.

St. John the Baptist Church has changed significantly over the decades, and even since Nasci wrote his article sixteen years ago. Some of the statuary, artwork, and locations he describes may differ from those seen by today's parishioners; and, while he laments the confinement of the Saints at that time, it should be noted that Saint John's has since added significant pieces to the Dominick Street church. These include the statue of the Blessed Mother that stands in the grotto outside the main entrance and a replica of The Pietà in the sanctuary. Several of the statues Nasci describes are again displayed in the sanctuary as well; a portrait of Christ inspired by the visions of St. Faustina Kowlaska, canonized in the year 2000, reflects the recent joining of St. John the Baptist Church with the traditionally Polish American Transfiguration of Our Lord Church.

The Catholic Mass has also changed considerably since the days of the immigrants. Shortly after St. John's moved to Dominick Street, Holy Mother Church implemented changes to the Mass following the Second Vatican Council. Mass is no longer said in Latin, and the celebrant now faces the congregation rather than 'ad orientem' (to the East), among other differences. One can sense Nasci's longing for the traditional Mass in his writing. His sentiments were shared by many of his generation; and, interestingly, a similar feeling is now expressed by a growing number of young Catholics who have found a new appreciation for the ancient ways. Thus is the beauty of the Catholic Church, transcending time and culture to unite the faithful worldwide, just as it did for those immigrants who first arrived in Rome, New York.

-Anthony J. Rotolo, Ph.D.

The faithful attending Mass at St. John the Baptist Church witness a ceremony in an ambience not unlike services and surroundings in other contemporary American Catholic churches. They worship in a bright interior, comfortably heated in winter and air-conditioned in summer, but the building's contemporary style, airy and light-filled nave is in stark contrast to the old church on River Street, a structure of impenetrable and somber aspect reminiscent of some Romanesque churches in the Old Country. The only reminder of old St. John's is the polychrome statue of the patron in the main entrance.

Anyone attending Mass in the old church would have seen him high above the main altar dominating the scene. His was a more impressive presence there. One was compelled to regard him as an integral part of the ceremony, especially in those days when the altar was against the wall of the apse and the celebrant faced with the congregation. Standing now in the entrance, closer to view, the statue appears diminished in size and lacks the symbolic power it evinced from its exalted place above the main altar. To gain a better sense of the visual and spiritual qualities of the old church and its old-world origins, one must visit the grotto of the new St. John's where statues and pictures of the saints that once adorned the walls and sculpture niches of the River Street structure are housed.

Confined to a few square feet of space behind a wrought iron railing are the several images that once held prominent positions in the nave of old St. John's. Gathered in the gloom, they wait for devotees to light a candle, say a prayer of thanksgiving, or plead for a favor while offering a promise in return for its concession. It was the way Italians related to the saints. They saw them as guardians and protectors and sometimes as intermediaries between themselves and the Almighty. The supplicants are fewer now. The custom of pleading for a favor—whether a cure for an illness, solution to a problem, or resolution of a family dispute—and promising a personal sacrifice or good work in return, is perhaps not so often done these days, but the sight of the faithful humbly standing or kneeling before a saint's image is characteristic of Italian Catholic observance and a reminder of the time when extensive banks of votive candles burned at the base of the statues in old St. John's with devotees of the immigrant generation, often women in severe widowhood black, praying before them.

The gallery of statues and paintings in the old church was an impressive sight. In their separate niches on each side of the outer aisles, they loomed over the congregation as if assuring the faithful they were there to hear their pleas and to intercede on their behalf. In our formative years we learned their names through church school, through our friends and classmates who knew them as their families' patrons, as well as through the annual festivals celebrated in their honor. We found ourselves awestruck by their mysterious images: the apparently dwarfish figure of St. Gregory in his miter and ecclesiastic robes; the Madonna Capocolonna with flames radiating outward from her entire figure; St. Lucy gazing ecstatically heavenward and holding a pair of eyes in her hand. Together with the others, their presence gripped the collective psyche of the faithful and was a constant reminder to the immigrant generation of the stone and stucco hillside towns, the old-world landscape, and the ancient culture left in the wake of Italian migration to the New World.

The patron saints held a place of great prominence then; not only physical prominence in their highly visible location, but also in the minds and hearts of the people who, in their singular form of Italian Catholicism, venerated the saints, developed intimate bonds with them, conversing with and beseeching them for what they were powerless to attain by themselves, while promising something in return. In the actual world one traded something of value for something of value, and so it was with Italians in relating to the saints. To them, the saints—especially the patron saints—had an actual presence in their daily lives: a presence felt in the effigies housed in local churches and chapels, in pictures and figurines found in homes, in the scapulars and medals they wore, and in the wallet-size pictures in their pockets. The saints' beneficial acts were not to be taken lightly. The faithful believed that the saints, like anyone else, would rightfully expect something in return for their good works. It was a very pragmatic relationship: you do something for me; I'll do something for you.

Return of a favor was generally made by fulfilling a vow: a resolution of fasting or abstinence, walking to a shrine on bare feet, naming a child after the saint, or making a sacrificial donation to a charity. In short, the vow was a verbal contract between the saint and the supplicant. The custom was scrupulously observed, and sometimes public recognition was given to commemorate the event. At some old-world shrines, *ex votos* were placed nearby the saint's effigy as evidence of a request granted: paintings illustrating the event, plaster limbs to indicate a physical cure, or other manifestations of favors received. Here, the most popular form of *ex voto* was the paid newspaper ad thanking a saint for a concession.

Besides the personal veneration of patrons, there were customary public observances as well: community prayers or special processions to relieve a drought or epidemic, or to further some other common cause; but the greatest occasion was an annual feast celebrated to honor the community's benefactor. As they did in the *paesi*, immigrants in the new land instituted the custom of celebrating feasts to commemorate patron saints: marvelous spectacles marked by Holy Mass, street processions, special holiday foods, and exciting field days crowned by dazzling firework displays. Wherever Italians settled in considerable numbers, they organized an annual festa, spurring a week-long outpouring of emotions toward their patron saint.

Here, at the old church, on the occasion of a village patron's feast, the observance was enhanced by placing the figure of the saint on a side altar directly before the congregation, to share the honor and solemnity of the sanctuary with the universal patron, St. John the Baptist. The spiritual climax of the festa came with the outdoor procession when the statue or painting of the patron being honored was placed on a palette and carried through the streets, borne on the shoulders of old country *paesani* honored by their sacred burden. Preceded by a band and an honor guard, with the saint's colorful banners flanked by the American and Italian flags, the bearers descended the steps and marched down the street with a throng of faithful in their wake; some carrying candles, others wearing scapulars, or fingering rosaries while reciting the prescribed prayers. The procession moved steadily down the street to Dominick Street where it turned toward East Rome, crossed the Mohawk River to Mill Street; and proceeded into the heart of the Italian neighborhood before retracing its path to St. John's.

Along the way devotees awaited the procession on porches and balconies draped with colorful linens and bedspreads. It was a custom transplanted from the Old Country. Bedding, the treasured hand-crafted products of a maiden's trousseau, was emblematic of the finest art that could embellish the home. On this day their decorative embroidery and lacework created a colorful passage for the patron and marchers. Occasionally, the marchers halted before some homes where prayers and litanies were recited exalting the patron, or occupants might individually praise the saint and give testimony to the efficacy of their prayers to him; meanwhile, people donated money which was pinned to streamers suspended from the figure or painting for this purpose. It was a tumultuous scene. The throng swelled with every step. As the parade went by, men doffed their hats and crossed themselves; many dropped to their knees momentarily and prayed, while others elbowed through the crowd to touch the figure or the special mantle adorning the saint on this occasion. And so, on they went with the band playing to a cacophony of fervent prayers, rosaries and hymns punctuated by spectators crying out *evvivas* all along the way.

Religious ardor manifested by the immigrants was a reflection of the pervasive role protective saints played in Italian life. Though there might be individual devotions to other saints, townsfolk collectively honored their appointed patron: it was the cohesive bond of the community, transcending even strict class differentiations found in Italian communes. Perhaps no other religious or secular holiday created the sense of community identification and pride as the patron's feast. This tradition crossed the seas with the townsfolk; though the immigrants were uprooted, there was a continuity of community spirit through their unswerving loyalty to the old-world saints as they continued their unique private and collective devotions to them.

Among the many sorrows Italians suffered through emigrating, one of their extreme regrets, along with leaving home, family, and neighbors, was removing themselves from the spiritual refuge of their protective overseers, the patron saints. This left a keenly sensed vacuum that endured in the new land. Undoubtedly, the memory and veneration of the hometown patron was one of the strongest cultural bonds between the immigrants and the *paese* they left behind. It was not unusual for an immigrant to carry a small picture of the village patron in a wallet or concealed in his clothing. Sometimes a bit of fabric from a mantle that once adorned the patron's statue would be carried or sewn into a garment lining as an amulet. This strong attachment to the saints and confidence in their guardianship was enduring. It continues to this day. Once, while a latter-day immigrant was describing his village's patron, he removed a frayed card from his wallet: it was a picture of St. Paul, his hometown patron. He had carried the card with him since leaving his home fifteen years before.

In the Old World, sometimes the only decorative element seen in the home was a picture of the patron saint, so it was demanding that a visual reminder of the ancestral village patron be displayed in Italian American homes. Romans from Raffadali, Sicily, generally displayed a picture of their patroness, *La Madonna degli Infermi*. The Madonna was noted for relieving a pestilence in the sixteenth century, and for her great mercy in curing the hopelessly ill, as well as for the mysterious circumstances surrounding the production of her statue and its arrival in Raffadali. Confidence in her powers was a cultural conditioning which carried across the sea, so that it wasn't unusual for elderly immigrants from Raffadali with several decades residence in America to beseech their ancestral patroness in the Old World for favors.

In popular Raffadalesi thought, the *Madonna degli Infermi* has always been their guardian, but history tells us otherwise. Before the Madonna, St. Oliva was the town's patroness. It was not unusual to exchange one patron for another if dissatisfied with the original saint's protection, or if the people felt a different saint might more effectively confront a new menace to the community.

St. Oliva was a ninth century martyr who, according to legend, was abducted by Saracens. She symbolized the Saracen era of Sicilian history and the subjection of Christians to Islamic rulers. Her fabled resistance to Saracen brutality continued to be a spiritual bulwark for Christians threatened by Muslim corsairs and raiders looking for plunder or involved in the lucrative slave trade centuries after the end of Saracen rule. St. Oliva's spiritual protection was bolstered by a coordinated warning and military response system which effectively squelched the raiders in time, but, with the threat of human depredation diminished, Mediterranean communities were assaulted by a more deadly foe. Sta. Oliva was seen as a safeguard against mankind, but something more powerful was needed to confront the waves of diseases carried to Europe from time to time; so, faced with a new and more devastating enemy, the Raffadalesi turned to the Madonna.

Firm in their belief that Mary had saved their community, the Raffadalesi adopted the Madonna as patroness; a festa was instituted; a new church, the Chiesa Madre, was built as her sanctuary; and a sculpture was commissioned to honor her. *La Madonna degli Infermi* is a polychrome woodcarving; the elongated figure of Mary nestles a restless Christ Child in her arms. The facial expressions and harmonious arrangement of forms reveal that it was no rustic carver who executed this exquisite piece; It was the work of an exceptionally skilled regional sculptor who conceived the subtle, half-smiling Virgin and countermovement in the beckoning Christ Child. Centuries later, his creation remains the community's precious jewel.

The sculptor was from Burgio, about forty-five miles away. A tree was selected for the work; and, when it was felled, a spring gushed from its roots that affected miraculous cures for those who drank its waters. Later, when the sculptor was halfway done, he returned to his task one morning to find the work completed by some unknown hand. The two miraculous events created a contention between the Burgitani and Raffadalesi for possession of the statue: the former claimed it because the events occurred in their town; the latter pressed their contractual rights. Ultimately, the Madonna was placed on an ox cart and drawn to a fork in the road where one arm led to Raffadali and the other to Burgio. Here the oxen were allowed to take their own direction. They chose the path leading to Raffadali and stopped in the middle of town where the Chiesa Madre was built to shelter her.

The Virgin Mother seems to have appealed to many Italian communes at one time or another for she is popular throughout Italy, as she is elsewhere in the Catholic world. Among the southern towns sending their sons and daughters to Rome, NY, there were at least four tutelary Madonnas. The proliferation of protective Madonnas in Italy very likely coincided with the phenomenon of Mary's ascendancy in the Church during the Gothic era. In France it is manifested in the many cathedrals dedicated to her, and in Italy through her adoption as patroness by numerous communities throughout the country.

San Egidio (St. Giles) is another saint whose patronage and legends have remained in the memory of some Romans. He was the old country patron of several Rome families who settled on the mucklands. Our older citizens will remember the thriving farms along lower South James Street. The fertile black soil was a marvel to motorists passing through Rome before the multi-laned arterial diverted traffic to the east. Produce stands were in abundance along the road in those days, and the farmers profited from their stands, as well as from periodically hauling crops to regional markets.

Reminiscing on her early years on South James Street, Josephine Grasso Mecca recalled how cars lined the roadside as motorists stopped to buy fresh vegetables from the "muck", as it was called, when she and her sisters assisted their parents in waiting on customers at the family's Stand. The Grassos, like several other muckland families, came from Linguaglossa in Sicily and settled first in nearby Canastota. There the Linguaglossesi were part of a colony established on truck farms cultivating vegetables for the Syracuse market; but when the 1918 Erie Canal was started and the Rome swamp drained, revealing a fertile soil, several Canastotans migrated to Rome. With their typical industriousness, these enterprising Italians developed the virgin land into the famous Rome muckland farms.

Their ancestral home, Linguaglossa, is a community on the northern slopes of Mt. Etna. *Mongibello*, as the Sicilians called Etna, was an insidious presence for all communities around it, with its untold eruptions and flaming rivers of lava destroying numerous villages and taking untold lives through the centuries; but Linguaglossa, according to its Paesani in America, never suffered the ravages of volcanic violence experienced by other Sicilian communes.

Josephine once asked her mother if she had been afraid of living so close to a volcano. Although her village was overshadowed by the mountain, and its perpetual fumes were a constant reminder of its awesome power, her mother professed no great fear: *"La fede ti salva"* (faith will save you), she replied. Hers was a complacency based on strong communal confidence in their protective saint, Egidio, who was their tireless guardian against the ever-threatening Mt. Eta. It was a faith based on record, as another member of the family, Joe Grasso, described the role of the saint as the town's protector: whenever the lava threatened, townsmen carried the statue of *San Egidio* from its sanctuary to the fields above the town. To the memory of its citizens, and to their undying gratitude, the town has always been spared. Joe's father told him of one occasion when the molten rock came dangerously close but was thwarted by the saint's effigy. As it approached his statue, the lava flow divided around him and away from the village.

Though his biography is scanty, *San Egidio* is an historical saint. Born about 700 A.D., he established a hermitage in a cave near the mouth of the Rhone River in France. Legendary accounts tell us he subsisted solely on doe's milk. Egidio was discovered accidently when the doe was pursued into the hermit's cave by hounds belonging to a king who eventually provided funds to found a monastery. After his death, there was a continually growing veneration of Egidio. In England alone, according to Butler's *Lives of the Saints*, some 160 churches were dedicated to him. In time he became venerated as the patron of cripples, beggars, and blacksmiths. His role as patron of cripples is seen in an illustration of a local legend: Etna fumes on the horizon; and in the foreground, a crippled woman is doomed until San Egidio appears, extends his crozier, and commands her to rise and walk.

Perhaps because they were not sufficiently numerous, immigrants from Raffadali and Linguaglossa never gained a highly visible identity through a mutual aid society or had an image of their hometown patron sent here; but people from other old world communities were; and, as they established themselves here in greater numbers and developed some affluence, they generated funds to obtain statues or paintings of their trusted patrons to grace their parish church and watch over them as they did in the Old World. As more and more immigrants came, the collection of statues and paintings grew. In time, St. John's housed several statues and paintings representing patron saints from various southern Italian towns.

Statuary at St. John's includes a St. Rocco, donated by people from Staletti in Calabria where they were parishioners of a church dedicated to him. Rocco is one of the most popular and beloved saints of Catholic Europe; and though he is an historical saint, and the main biographical data are known, it did not prevent his factual life from being enmeshed with folklore. Born in Montpelier, France, in the early fourteenth century, Roch (Rocco) was a pious and compassionate Christian on pilgrimage to Rome when he arrived at a plague-ridden town. Undaunted, he remained to care for the victims, ministering to them however he could in their horrible final hours. He continued on pilgrimage, halting at other places afflicted by the dreaded "black death" of that era, and attending to its unfortunate victims before pressing on to Rome, which he found decimated by the disease and virtually abandoned. Returning to France, he again encountered plague in town after town where he mercifully cared for the sick and assisted in the grim task of burying the dead.

Exposed so often to the malady, Rocco eventually contracted the plague himself and, unwilling to burden others, went off to a forest to await death alone. At this point, according to pious lore, death was circumvented by a dog who brought Rocco a nourishing loaf of bread daily until he was able to resume his journey. The effects of plague and rigors of his protracted pilgrimage disfigured Rocco so badly that he was unrecognizable to his fellow townsmen on his return. Suspected of being a spy, he was thrown into prison where he soon perished. His sanctity was revealed when, upon discovering his body, the jailer reported an unearthly light shining in the cell. Eventually, other stories were told of an angel leaving a tablet in the cell confirming that Rocco was a saint.

As a survivor of the plague, and compassionate minister to its victims, the saint's cult spread widely through Europe; in time, Roche, the Frenchman whose great piety compelled him to wander in pilgrimage, became endeared to Italians as *San Rocco*. To them, St. Rocco represented formidable power in overcoming the most feared disease of medieval times. Being associated with someone thus favored could be a safeguard against the scourge that destroyed nearly half of Europe's population. With such credentials, the fourteenth century pilgrim was adopted by hundreds of European communities as their patron.

St. Rocco's statue in St. John's grotto follows some of the imagery developed from the saint's legend. Dressed in a cinctured robe and short cape, he carries a staff with a drinking gourd attached and a pouch slung from his shoulder. Scallop shells on his cape and hat identify Rocco as a pilgrim. Since his likeness was unknown, Rocco was generally given the accepted features of Christ or St. James (St. John's Rocco is apparently the latter). The saint points to a wound in his thigh: the symbol of the plague. In contemporary imagery, the black death was visualized as a storm of arrows punishing mankind for their sins. But St. John's statue is not representative of all St. Rocco statuary: as his cult grew, there were several variations of this imagery. In some works, he points to a "bubo" on his thigh, rather than a wound. This was the actual swelling symptom of Bubonic Plague. In other statuary, the dog is missing, perhaps because this folkloric episode of Rocco's life was unknown in the sculptor's locale. Some sculptures have an angel standing by; while in paintings, the angel might be hovering and closing the wound with his fingertips. The many variations attest to the widespread popularity of San

Rocco's cult, for wherever the carving or painting was done, it was with current local knowledge of the saint and accepted representational elements in mind.

The Toccolana Club displays a painting of *San Eustachio*, the patron of Tocco da Casauria, the old-world home of the organization's founders in Abruzzo. Eustachio (Eustace) is pictured with his family being menaced by a lion, tiger, and leopard in an arena while an angel, clutching a palm branch, the symbol of martyrdom, hovers overhead. The saint bravely confronts the wild beasts with arms outstretched, shielding his terrified wife and children as sanguine spectators in the background scream for the cats to begin their savage work. But the animals hesitate; the lion and tiger stand still while the leopard skulks in the background. In spite of the angel and palm, it is not the moment of this Christian family's martyrdom; rather, it is their miraculous triumph in the arena when the beasts refused to attack. Dated 1950, the painting appears to be from the brush of an unschooled artist; a product of folk art similar to pictorial ex votos seen elsewhere in Catholic shrines and sanctuaries. Wedged between the frame and painting are several memorial cards commemorating deceased members of the Toccolana Club and symbolizing the devotion of old-timer Toccolani to their protective saint. On the lower right, the artists signature, M. Stromei, echoes a family name here, as well as one of Tocco da Casauria's past illustrious citizens, the shoemaker-poet, Domenico Stromei.

A full-length portrait of San Eustachio as a Roman soldier was also displayed in the grotto at St. John's. It shows a stag with a crucifix extending upward from its head standing beside him. The recorded legend of St. Eustace described by Butler tells us that Placidus, an accomplished Roman general during Trajan's reign, was hunting one day when a stag approached him with a crucifix mounted between its antlers. The impaled Christ called to Placidas from the cross, and the awestruck soldier immediately converted to the new faith together with his wife and sons. He changed his name to Eustachius and left the army to follow a Christian life. In time, he was called upon to lead Roman forces against barbarians threatening the Empire; but, following his triumphant return, enraged the emperor by refusing to pay homage to pagan gods. Eustachius was subsequently ordered to face the lions in the arena. Frustrated by the lions' unusual timidity before the undaunted Christian soldier, Trajan was not to be denied his vengence, nor was Eustachius to be thwarted in achieving martyrdom: the emperor directed that Eustachius and his family be placed in a brazen bull and roasted alive.

The patron of Tocco da Casauria stands alone as a soldier among the Madonnas, ecclesiastic saints, and other patrons in St. John's collection. The church dedicated to him in Tocca da Casauria was constructed early in the thirteenth century, and his adoption as the town's patron came when a warrior saint would be most fitting as community protector. Situated in Abruzzo, on a route traveled by forces contending for regional control throughout its long history, Tocco da Casauria roads felt the heels of numerous armies on the march: Roman, Byzantine, Lombard, Norman, German, Swabian, and Angevin troops passed through before the thirteenth century ended. As the church dedicated to San Eustachio was being constructed, Frederick II, Holy Roman Emperor, and King of Sicily, seeking to consolidate his peninsular domain, ordered a fortress castle built in Tocco da Casauria to guard its strategic position between the hinterland and the sea. It was a time of constant strife with rapacious armies afield threatening the land and its people. According to Toccolano lore, the soldier-martyr, whose cult was flourishing during this era, was invoked at a decisive moment in battle when the local forces, with "Viva San Eustachio" as their battle cry, routed the enemy.

The San Eustachio legend is embellished by Toccolano folklore. Antonetta de Angelo Zaccardi came here from Abruzzo in 1928 with her husband and infant daughter, Marianina. Over the years, she imparted the village lore to her children and grandchildren. Her recollection of the San Eustachio legend reflects the local color of oral tradition. Unlike written accounts that attempted to authenticate events in a specific time and place, local stories of patron saints were generally accepted on faith. To the folk, events were the important stuff, not the where or when. According to Antonetta, Eustachio was a pagan who persecuted Christians and scorned the Savior they followed. Once he was hunting in the forest and, frustrated in finding no game, cursed the Lord and vowed that the first thing he saw, even if it were Gesú Cristo Himself, was going to be "bagged". Soon after, a stag approached, and Eustachio prepared to strike; but he paused when he noticed a crucifix mounted between its antlers. Seeing Christ nailed to the cross, Eustachio repented; he dropped to his knees, began to weep, and begged the Lord's forgiveness for persecuting Christians and denying the Savior. Thereafter, Eustachio, his wife and sons became devout Christians, enduring the ridicule and oppression other faithful had formerly suffered at his hands. In time, he and his family were condemned to death and ordered into a bronze bull. A fire was kindled beneath it, and the pious family were on their way to martyrdom; but, certain of redemption and happy to sacrifice their lives for the faith, they perished while singing joyful hymns in praise of the Lord.

Of the several old-world patrons represented in the church here, the Madonna Capocolonna and San Gregorio, patroness and patron of the Calabrian towns of Crotone and Staletti on the Ionian Sea, are probably the best known. Several Romans are acquainted with the local folklore surrounding the two. Recent immigrants from these communities indicate that the legends are still told in the old paesi. The following legend of the Madonna Capocolonna is from Elvira Securra Desantis, who came here as a young girl from Crotone. Her story recalls the ominous presence of the Turk in Italian history and folklore. In popular thought, "Turk" was synonymous with "heathen," and conjured a terrifying image of rapacious piracy. The Turk was the bogeyman for children in southern Italian coastal towns. Elvira reminisced on her mother's warnings about Turkish marauders kidnapping children to enslave or hold them for ransom—an event that actually occurred in past eras, and a theme that found its way into scenarios of the popular Italian Commedia delle Arte of past centuries. Thus, though the Crotone legend takes place in some undetermined time, the cultural background lends credence to it.

Elvira related that Turkish raiders had pillaged Crotone and collected a hoard of booty, including the town's treasured icon of the Madonna Capocolonna. Hoping to locate this beautiful lady with the aid of the painting, the raiders took it aboard ship and prepared to sail; however, when they weighed anchor, the ship failed to move. Thinking their vessel was too heavily laden, they jettisoned some of their loot. Still, they could not move. They unburdened the ship again, but still without result. The raiders were reluctant to abandon the Madonna's icon since they expected to be rewarded by the Sultan should they find her for his harem. Ultimately, the raiders determined that the Madonna was a powerful sorceress and attempted to break her spell by putting a torch to her image. It ignited momentarily, but the flames soon died out. Our storyteller insists that the Madonna allowed the infidel Turks to set her image afire in order to demonstrate her power over their efforts to destroy her. Nevertheless, the fumes darkened her features. "That is why she is a black Madonna," Elvira declared. Finally, the Turkish raiders, overwhelmed by her display of power, threw the painting overboard and the ship moved out to sea.

The Crotonesi regretted losing their personal possessions, but grieved the tragic loss of their precious icon. Unknown to them, the painting drifted toward the Capo delle Colonne, a promontory named for the remaining columns of a classical ruin. As it neared shore, it was discovered by a recluse who took it to his shoreside hovel nearby, hoping to realize a fortune in selling it later. Soon after, he fell mortally ill and called for a priest who performed last rites and heard the poor man's confession. He revealed the location of the painting, expired with a clear conscience, and the Madonna Capocolonna was restored to its sanctuary in Crotone. Annually, the Crotonesi celebrate a feast to commemorate the Madonna's return to her rightful place. Her icon is taken in procession to the Cape of the Columns by land and returned by sea in a small boat, followed by a flotilla in procession to her sanctuary in Crotone. A dedicatory prayer glorifies her as the *"bruna e bella Signora di Capocolonna"* (dark and beautiful lady of the Cape of Columns) who, in taking the name of the Cape, replaced the pagan gods once worshiped there: *"Un tempo, sede di Divinita' false e bugiarde"* (once the place of false and deceitful gods).

The Crotonese Madonna is similar to many other representations of the Virgin Mary elsewhere in the Catholic world. There are several black or dark Madonnas, including the famous Virgin of Guadalupe and Virgin of Montserrat in Spain, and Our Lady of Czestochowa in Poland. Other similarities are seen in the derivation and arrangement of forms and elements in the work: the circle of stars about her head, and flames radiating from the figure are seen in numerous representations of Mary; and, in paintings where the lower extremities are visible, she stands upon a crescent. The imagery is derived from the Apocalypse of St. John the Apostle (Revelation) 12:1, which proclaims:

And a great sign appeared in heaven: A woman clothed with the sun, and the moon under her feet, and on her head a crown of twelve stars.

Children at Mass in the River Street Church would shrink from the fearful image of Saint Gregory. Nine o'clock Mass was scheduled for the parish children then; and, led by Parish Visitor sisters, the young worshipers recited prayers in unison as Saint Gregory glared down from his niche overhead. It is a vivid memory for many of Rome's Italian-Americans who would confess to the feeling of dread that *San Gregorio Taumaturgo* inspired in them.

Saint Gregory was a third century bishop of Neocaesarea in Asia Minor. His surname, Taumaturgo (the Wonderworker), might have been owing to his missionary zeal; but, more likely, he earned it through legendary powers he demonstrated in the Lord's name: he moved great rocks, diverted rivers, and drained bodies of water. Sources tend to confuse Gregory the Wonderworker with Gregory the Enlightener. Both have been recognized for carrying the faith to Armenia, though the Armenians credit their conversion to Gregory the Enlightener and honor him as their patron. Regardless, the remains of both saints ended up in Italy. Gregory the Enlightener is venerated by Neapolitans who claim to have his relics. On the other hand, Gregory the Wonderworker's remains, Stalettian legend tells us, found their way to the Calabrian shore by some mysterious means and were enshrined there.

The dwarfish figure of Saint Gregory in the grotto might be puzzling to a viewer unaware of the local legend. From the viewpoint of at least one child of the 1930s, he seemed to be kneeling beneath those heavy robes; but the legend reveals something else: Gregory's body was discovered with its legs severed, which the statue's ecclesiastic garment graciously conceals. At least two variations of the Stalettian legend came here with the immigrants: one told by Rosalia Mosca, who left her homeland in 1928; the other is shared by Joseph Griffo Sr., who emigrated in 1937.

According to Rosalia Mosca, Gregory was captured by pirates who murdered him, mutilated his body, stuffed it into a crate and tossed it overboard. The crate drifted toward Calabria, finally washing ashore near Staletti where it was soon covered by shifting sands and remained hidden until found by a hunter years later. A strange series of events then led to the unearthing of Gregory's remains. A hunter occasionally passed by the shore where the saint's body was buried; and each time he approached the site, his dogs barked and yelped excitedly, and ran off to the crate's exact location, pawing furiously in the ground until the master whistled for them to return. The animals repeated their frantic clawing whenever in the area, removing more and more sand until the hunter called them off.

Eventually, the dogs' fascination with the spot aroused the master's interest, so he allowed them to follow their natural urge while satisfying his own piqued curiosity. The hunter watched, dumbfounded, as his dogs pawed sand into the air and exposed the crate. Perhaps he thought it was the realization of every southern Italian's dream: the discovery of a Turk's or brigand's buried treasure. He urged the dogs on until the container was fully revealed, then called them off while he examined it. He found an inscription on the crate, miraculously preserved despite the effects of saltwater, abrasive sand, and time. It identified the remains, now reduced to bone, as those of Gregory, a pious servant of God, gave instructions to provide a proper resting place for his relics, and ordered that a monastery be raised on the site of their discovery. The hunter revealed his discovery to his fellow Stalettians, and construction of an abbey was soon underway. Gregory's bones were encased in a glass reliquary and installed in the altar of the church. Since then, Saint Gregory has worked all kinds of wondrous miracles, but is best known for his ability to expel evil. His devotees believed if anyone were possessed by demonic spirits, Saint Gregory could be invoked for help. A pilgrimage to his shrine was said to exorcise any evil or lingering stain sin.

Joe Griffo's version of the legend involves a mysterious cat that stood by the beached crate until someone happened by. When the crate was opened, revealing the saint's relics, the cat stalked off into a nearby grotto and followed a long subterranean passage to Staletti. The townsfolk interpreted the animal's strange actions as a sign that Gregory's remains should be enshrined there; and a church was erected to house the holy relics. A feast was then inaugurated to commemorate the event. Every November 17th the saint's image is taken by motorcade to the shore where a procession of small craft accompanies it to the grotto site which is inaccessible by land.

To the Stalettians, Gregory the Wonderworker was certainly aptly named. In addition to personal miracles, Gregory favored the community with the same auspicious power over nature demonstrated in his early history, time and again interceding for dire community needs. Rosalia Moasca remembered the times her beloved San Gregorio Taumaturgo relieved terrible droughts when his statue was borne in solemn procession through the town and into the parched fields with hopes he would intervene to remove the specter of famine haunting the area under such circumstances. Joe Griffo described a prodigious event that gave rise to an annual celebration: *"Il giorno del miracle"* (the day of the miracle), when Staletti's exalted patron was placed on a promontory to confront an oncoming storm. He calmed the violent winds and seas and saved the town. Since then, May 13th, has been a local holiday commemorating the event.

Special processions and other public observances to overcome a common danger were not rare events in old country towns where the people, having meager weapons to battle disease, drought, storms and other threats to their well-being, saw their protective saint as the ultimate means of salvation. In their basic economy, a storm or drought threatening grainfields, orchards, and vineyards could be the difference between sustenance and starvation. So desperate were some situations that people would scourge themselves during processions and prayer gatherings to arouse the pity of the patron, and effigies of saints were sometimes left in the fields to "experience" what the people were suffering.

Repetition of specific motifs in the saints' stories should surprise no one. Saints lived unique lives, and martyrs suffered uniquely horrible tortures and executions which became their trademarks, so to speak; but it is not unusual to find elements transposed from one saint's legend to another. The crucifix between the antlers of a stag in the St. Eustace legend appears in St. Hubert's and others, and doe's milk was nourishment for the hermit. San Calogero, patron of Agrigento, as well as for San Egidio. Among the local legends discussed above, the *Madonna Capocolonna* of Crotone and *Madonna degli Infermi* of Raffadali have a common motif in the miraculous completion of their effigies. Like the Burgitano sculptor, the anonymous painter of the Crotone Madonna retired from his work one night, leaving only the head of the Christ Child unfinished. He returned the next morning to find it completed. These are but a few of many commonly used motifs found not only in Italian saint lore, but also in saint stories and legends throughout Christianity.

As in the *San Rocco* and *San Gregorio* legends, a dog appears in a story about San Vito. Dogs appear often in saints' legends as a compassionate creature and reflection of the charitable saint himself. Similarly, a dog plays this role in the pious lore of *San Vito* (St. Vitus), as shared by Josephine Tardugno, who came to America in 1911. Like all Italians, she landed here with few tangible goods and a wealth of folklore from her village, Rionero in Vulture, in mountainous Basilicata. She related that San Vito was gravely wounded, alone, without help and about to die until a kindly dog appeared, tenderly licked his wounds, and watched over him until he recovered. To show his gratitude, *San Vito* asked the Lord to provide him with a special reward for his canine benefactor; and the Lord responded by sending a loaf of bread for the dog. This, Josephine said, was the origin of bread: a Divine gift to reward for the dog's charity.

Sadly, the immigrant experience in Rome, NY, also entails the passing of once traditional events instituted by the immigrants. Rome has perhaps seen its last street procession, passion play, and other traditional observances. The immigrant's descendants, prone to reminisce on their "good old days", recall family cohesiveness, and the nurturing benefits of supportive priests, sisters, and teachers, as well as the Boy Scouts of America, YMCA and other institutions contributing to their development as they groped for an identity their formative years. They sometimes wonder why so many facets of their old-world culture disappeared.

Romans from Avigliano in Basilicata were among the most vigorous Italians in the community. Their cohesiveness was evidenced by the organization of a mutual aid society, maintenance of an activity hall where social and cultural functions took place, donation of the *Madonna del Carmine* (Our Lady of Mt. Carmel, patroness of their homeland village) to St. John's statuary, and the institution of an annual festa in her honor. Nevertheless, this spirited group witnessed the dissolution of the society, abandonment of the Aviglianese Hall, and the end of public celebrations honoring their patroness as the torch was passed to the next generation. The *Madonna del Carmine*, with a few votive candles glowing at her feet, is perhaps the only tangible evidence of this once-flourishing organization. She and the other figures remain at St. John's as visual reminders of the vibrant Italian American history of our city.

Laura Nardozza Lupica, daughter of Aviglianesi immigrants, discussed her thoughts on the gradual termination of local festas and public devotions to their patroness. She raised the issue of the growing difficulty street processions posed for increased traffic on Dominick Street, but also suggested that the underlying reason for phasing-out the colorful folkway was attributable to the collective attitude of indifference among American-born Italians toward these events. As they matured and became more conscious of their American identities, the new generation developed a disinterest in street processions and other Italianate Catholic practices, viewing them as anachronistic old world customs, out of place in their modern lives.

To the above, add a continually weakened identity with the *paese* through the gradual passing of the immigrant generation, the marriage of their children with those from other provinces and regions, and the dispersal of Italians from ethnic enclaves into other neighborhoods and other parishes. Moreover, their children were enculturated in public schools and other institutions into "the melting pot," and many Italian Americans entered adulthood during World War II, a period when all ethnic Americans were united in common cause and after which tens of thousands of Italian American veterans attended colleges and universities, wading deeper into the American mainstream.

When the new St. John the Baptist opened its doors in 1953, the old-world saints were no longer in view. They were taken from their honored places in the old church nave and housed in a crypt beneath the sanctuary of the new structure. Going from the old to the new, St. John the Baptist Church traveled only a few hundred yards in space, but moved centuries in time, from a style essentially Romanesque to one of contemporary design. In the former building, the saints' galleries were integral architectural elements formed by overhangs of the exterior wall, creating an interior with unimpeded outer aisles where the faithful could light candles and make private devotions to their trusted patrons. Planners perhaps felt that accommodating these venerations in the new structure would compromise design integrity; or perhaps they had an eye on construction costs which soared in the post-war era. Possibly, authorities perceived a waning interest in the saints, yet, reluctant to disregard some parishioners' spiritual needs, settled on housing the images in the basement crypt. It seemed a reasonable solution, but some had misgivings. Discussing this question, an older parishioner whose family had donated a painting of their old country patron, inferred that that the saints were no longer wanted inside the church. Though not universal, it was a sentiment shared by many of his generation who felt the saints had become more confined than enshrined.

The saints and observances surrounding them were the visual aspects of religion that stimulated Italian sensibilities, characterized their Catholicism and, while veneration of the old-world patrons is waning and the pageantry honoring them is past, they are reminders of a time when their lives and legends created a bond among Italians here and motivated them in cooperative efforts toward common goals. Barring unforeseen revivals and given the erosion of Italian cultural values concurrent with continual assimilation, public religious celebrations and emphasis on local patron saints will remain a thing of the past—an historical episode in Rome's Italian American experience.

Meanwhile, the patrons' images can still be found at St. John's, and they are still visited by a few surviving immigrants and second-generation Americans imbued with Italian Catholic values gained in their early years. A few candles are lit from time to time with an accompanying jingle of coins in the collection box, followed by prayers of thanksgiving or supplication. Once, extensive racks of candles created warm, moving reflections from the polychrome statues that contrasted with the solemn devotees standing or kneeling at their feet. Is it only a matter of time until these ancient old-world guardians see the last candle burning before them?

VISITING THE PARISH VISITORS

Anthony J. Rotolo, Ph.D.

Sr. Mary Gemma, Sr. Mylene Rosemarie, Sr. Susan Marie, Sr. Joan Germaine

For nearly 75 years, St. John the Baptist Church was blessed by the presence and service of the Parish Visitors of Mary Immaculate. During that time, the sisters were an integral and vibrant part of our community; and, through their countless contributions, they touched the lives of every parishioner and many more throughout our city.

In their humble black or dark blue habits, the Parish Visitors were a constant presence at Mass. Kneeling in silent prayer, they would smile warmly to greet families as they arrived. The sisters especially adored children, and the feeling was mutual. They were our teachers for religious education, first Holy Communion, and Confirmation. We looked up to them with awe for their vocation; and we knew each sister by name.

Every child of St. John's had a favorite sister. For me, it was Sr. Mary Cepha Euell, my second grade "Church school" teacher. Small in stature at no more than five feet tall, she nonetheless filled any room with her ever-present smile. Defying the old stereotype of the stern teacher-nun, Sr. Mary Cepha radiated with a childlike spirit. Her eyes were filled with curiosity and wonder, as if she saw every day and each person as a gift to be cherished.

I can still remember the day that Sr. Mary Cepha taught us to pray the Rosary. She was jubilant as she passed out a colorful assortment of beads to capture her young students' attention. I chose a glow-in-the-dark Rosary; and, as I held it up, Sister's eyes sparked with an excitement that matched my own. She sat beside me and the other children, cupping her hands around the beads to see them glow, and began to explain how each bead represented a prayer.

The sisters also enjoyed spending time with the older children of our parish. Sr. Mary Cepha would often hang out with the teens at CYO to help with our service activities. At that age, we had many questions about her life and religious vocation that she was always pleased to answer. Many wanted to know what her name meant, and she would proudly share that "Cepha" was a reference to St. Peter, the first Pope, who was called "Cephas" (rock) by Jesus. At CYO meetings, Sister especially liked to play games, make crafts, and share snacks—she had a notorious sweet tooth, in fact. We caught her many times "sneaking" into the kitchen for a treat as we fried donuts to serve after Sunday Mass.

In many ways, Sr. Mary Cepha embodied the words of her order's foundress, Mother Mary Teresa Tallon, who once said, "God expects

Rose Mattia and Sr. Mary Cepha, May 15, 2014

us to have a good community life, to pray well, to work faithfully, and to play cheerfully." The same was true of Sr. Mary Elise, Sr. Mary Josita, and all the Parish Visitors who served at St. John's. They tirelessly and cheerfully taught faith formation, sang in the choir, led prayer groups, and, most importantly, organized charity programs for those in need. The Parish Visitors were known throughout the region for the assistance they provided to all who were poor, sick, troubled, or alone in our community.

The following story, shared with me by Anna Anania of Rome, beautifully illustrates how the Parish Visitors' mission touched the lives of parishioners, often in unseen ways. At the time of this writing, Anna is 88 years old and has attended Mass at St. John's all her life. When she was a child, Anna and her mother, Elizabetta, would walk "from East Whitesboro Street, down Bouck Street, to River Street" every Sunday. When her mother passed away suddenly, young Anna faithfully continued walking to Mass by herself every week, and her situation was soon noticed by the sisters there.

"One day, Sister Mary Veronica took me to the convent," Anna remembered. "She sewed a kerchief for me because I didn't wear anything on my head." Later, the

Mother Carole Marie and Theresa Holmes

Parish Visitors helped Anna develop her own sewing skills. "I went to Catholic Charities," which was run by the Parish Visitors at that time, and "Sister Mary Veronica taught me how to do the blind stitch." The sisters blessed Anna's life in many ways, as did another kind woman she met one day as she walked. "Her name was Julia Strange, and she showed me how to use a sewing machine," Anna said. "She always had a smile for me, and we never forgot" about the Parish Visitors. The two remained lifelong friends until Julia's passing in 2018 at the age of 93.

"My sister and I always told our mom that she would have been a great nun," Julia's son, Nick Strange, recalled. He and his sister, Mary (Strange) Fahey, accompanied their mother on several trips to visit the Parish Visitors at Marycrest, the order's motherhouse in Monroe, New York. Situated on a picturesque hilltop, Marycrest houses a novitiate and formation center, infirmary, and administrative offices from which they presently conduct missions in

the United States, Nigeria, and the Philippines.

Visits to Marycrest were once a frequent part of parish life at St. John's. Organized for many years by my grandmother, Marie Rotolo, and Teresa Holmes, the bus trips were a favorite event for the sisters and parishioners, including the Strange family. "My mother was in her glory and hugged every sister she met," Nick Strange remembered. "We were always greeted with smiles from the sisters, welcoming their friends from Rome."

Departing early in the morning from St. John's, parishioners would journey four hours to Marycrest for a day that included Mass, lunch, and praying the Rosary. The visit also allowed them to reconnect with the sisters who had retired to the motherhouse after decades of service at St. John's. Nick Strange especially enjoyed capturing these moments with his camera. "The sisters always beamed when I would take their photos and videos," he remembered. Nick kindly provided the images for this article.

These pilgrimages took on even

Sr. Joan Germaine and Nick Strange

**May 15, 2014, Sr. Mary Elise with
Mary Fahey, Julia Strange and Anna Anania**

greater importance when, in 2009, we received word that the Parish Visitors would be ending their mission at St. John's just as our parish marked its centennial anniversary. The news was met with great sadness as many struggled to imagine our parish without the sisters. "This was not a decision that we reached easily," said Sr. Carole Marie, then the general superior of the order. Noting that religious vocations had been declining since the 1960s, she asked for prayers and understanding as our four remaining Parish Visitors—Sr. Mary Gemma, Sr. Joan Germaine Riley, Sr. Mylene Rosemarie, and Sr. Susan Marie—returned to Marycrest for reassignment. The absence of the Parish Visitors is still felt profoundly at St. John's. The sisters kneeling in quiet contemplation before mass is just a memory for a congregation whose children no longer benefit from their presence as role models of religious vocation. Faith formation is now taught by laypeople, as is increasingly common at Catholic churches, and charity work is organized by volunteers. Members of our community no longer see the sisters walking in their dark habits, so often worn with frayed edges reflecting their solemn vow of poverty; nor can Romans visit the convent house where the sisters lived. At the time of this writing, bus trips to Marycrest have also ceased.

St. John's has not forgotten the Parish Visitors, however; nor will we ever. It is my hope that the sisters and all who read this article will know of our gratitude for the many ways they enriched our church, families, and spiritual lives. At Mass, we pray often for religious vocations. In our hearts, we also pray for the day that the Parish Visitors of Mary Immaculate return to Rome, New York, for another mission at St. John the Baptist & Transfiguration of Our Lord.

Sr. Mary Gemma, Sr. Maria Catherine, Sister Mary Josita

May 12, 2016 · Sr. Linda Jean Marie and Sister Susan Marie

May 12, 2016 - Sr. Linda Jean Marie and Teresa Holmes

Sister Maria Catherine and Sr. Theresa Marie

Praying the Holy Rosary

"The rosary is the book of the blind, where souls see and there enact the greatest drama of love the world has ever known; it is the book of the simple, which initiates them into mysteries and knowledge more satisfying than the education of other men; it is the book of the aged, whose eyes close upon the shadow of this world and open on the substance of the next. The power of the rosary is beyond description."

Venerable Archbishop Fulton Sheen

The Holy Rosary is one of the oldest and most popular prayer traditions shared by Catholics around the world. The origins of its practice date back to the earliest days of the Church when, according to historical records, Christians began using strings of beads for prayer and meditation. By the Middle Ages, these beads were commonly used to count a series of Our Father prayers and thus became known by their Latin name, Paternosters.

The Rosary evolved over many centuries until the Rosarium, or "rose garden," took on its familiar form in the 11th Century A.D. According to Catholic tradition, the Blessed Virgin Mary appeared to St. Dominic, presenting him with a string of Rosary beads and asking him to pray 15 Our Fathers and 150 "Angelic Salutations," referring to the words spoken to her by the Archangel Gabriel from which the Hail Mary prayer is derived. These prayers were grouped into 15 "decades," each representing an Our Father and ten Hail Mary prayers.

Blessed Virgin Mary presents the Rosary to St. Dominic.

The Mother of God asked St. Dominic to pray the Rosary while meditating on a series of mysteries associated with each decade. These mysteries recount the Incarnation, Passion, Death and Resurrection of her Son, Jesus Christ.

Our Lady repeated her request to pray the Rosary when she appeared to three children in Fatima, Portugal, in 1917. The Blessed Virgin asked the children to pray the Rosary every day to bring peace to the world. She then taught them to include the Fatima Prayer after each decade. Many Catholics have since adopted the practice of saying the Fatima Prayer as part of the Rosary.

Today, the Rosary is commonly understood to consist of 59 beads divided into five decades; however, many Catholics pray a full Rosary of 15 decades daily, as requested by Our Lady.

HOW TO PRAY THE ROSARY

1. Make the *Sign of the Cross*
2. Pray the *Apostles' Creed*
3. Pray the *Our Father*
4. Pray the *Hail Mary* three (3) times for the virtues of Faith, Hope, and Charity
5. Pray the *Glory Be*
6. Announce the first Mystery (see below)
7. Pray the *Our Father*
8. Pray the *Hail Mary* ten (10) times while meditating on the Mystery
9. Pray the *Glory Be* followed by the *Fatima Prayer*
10. Announce the next Mystery; then repeat steps (7 through 9) as you continue through the remaining Mysteries
11. Pray the *Hail Holy Queen* and Closing Prayer
12. Make the *Sign of the Cross*

MYSTERIES OF THE HOLY ROSARY

The Joyful Mysteries (Monday and Saturday)
The Annunciation to Mary
The Visitation of Mary
The Birth of our Lord Jesus Christ
The Presentation of the Child Jesus in the Temple
The Finding of Our Lord in the Temple

The Sorrowful Mysteries (Tuesday and Friday)
The Agony of Christ in the Garden
The Scourging at the Pillar
The Crowning with Thorns
The Carrying of the Cross
The Crucifixion and Death of Our Lord on the Cross

The Luminous Mysteries (Thursday)
The Baptism of Our Lord in the Jordan
The Wedding at Cana
The Proclamation of the Kingdom
The Transfiguration of Our Lord
The Institution of the Eucharist

Glorious Mysteries (Wednesday and Sunday)
The Resurrection of Our Lord
The Ascension of Our Lord
The Descent of the Holy Spirit upon the Apostles
The Assumption of the Mary into Heaven
The Coronation of Mary as Queen of Heaven & Earth

PRAYERS OF THE ROSARY

....

in English and Latin

Sign of the Cross

In the name of the Father, and of the Son, and of the Holy Spirit. Amen.

In nomine Patris et Filii et Spiritus Sancti. Amen.

Apostles' Creed

I believe in God the Father Almighty, Creator of heaven and earth; and in Jesus Christ, His only Son, our Lord; Who was conceived by the Holy Spirit, born of the Virgin Mary, suffered under Pontius Pilate, was crucified, died, and was buried. He descended into hell; the third day He rose again from the dead; He ascended into heaven, and is seated at the right hand of God, the Father Almighty; from there He shall come to judge the living and the dead.

I believe in the Holy Spirit, the holy Catholic Church, the communion of saints, the forgiveness of sins, the resurrection of the body, and life everlasting.

Amen.

Credo in Deum, Patrem omnipotentem, creatorem caeli et terrae. Et in Iesum Christum, Filium eius unicum, Dominum nostrum, qui conceptus est de Spiritu Sancto, natus ex Maria Virgine, passus sub Pontio Pilato, crucifixus, mortuus et sepultus. Descendit ad inferos, tertia die resurrexit a mortuis. Ascendit ad caelos, sedet ad dextram Dei Patris omnipotentis. Inde venturus est iudicare vivos et mortuos.

Credo in Spiritum Sanctum, sanctam Ecclesiam catholicam, sanctorum communionem, remissionem peccatorum, carnis resurrectionem, vitam aeternam.

Amen.

Our Father (Pater Noster)

Our Father, Who art in heaven, hallowed be Thy name, Thy kingdom come; Thy will be done on earth as it is in heaven.

Give us this day our daily bread; and forgive us our trespasses, as we forgive those who trespass against us. And lead us not into temptation; but deliver us from evil.

Amen.

Pater noster, qui es in caelis: Sanctificetur nomen tuum: Adveniat regnum tuum: Fiat voluntas tua, sicut in caelo, et in terra.

Panem nostrum quotidianum da nobis hodie: Et dimitte nobis debita nostra, sicut et nos dimittimus debitoribus nostris. Et ne nos inducas in tentationem, sed libera nos a malo

Amen.

Hail Mary (Ave Maria)

Hail, Mary, full of grace; the Lord is with thee; blessed art thou among women, and blessed is the fruit of thy womb, Jesus.

Holy Mary, Mother of God, pray for us sinners, now and at the hour of our death.

Amen.

Ave Maria, gratia plena: Dominus tecum, benedicta tu in mulieribus, et benedictus fructus ventris tui, Iesus.

Sancta Maria, Mater Dei, ora pro nobis peccatoribus, nunc et in hora mortis nostrae.

Amen.

Fatima Prayer

O my Jesus, forgive us our sins, save us from the fires of hell, and lead all souls to heaven, especially those in most need of Thy mercy.

Domine Iesu, dimitte nobis debita nostra, salva nos ab igne inferiori, perduc in caelum omnes animas, praesertim eas quae misericordiae tuae maximae indigent.

Hail Holy Queen (Salve, Regina)

Hail, Holy Queen, Mother of mercy, our life, our sweetness and our hope. To thee do we cry, poor banished children of Eve. To thee to we send up our sighs, mourning and weeping in this valley of tears. Turn, then, most gracious advocate, thine eyes of mercy toward us; and after this, our exile, show unto us the blessed fruit of thy womb, Jesus. O clement, O loving, O sweet Virgin Mary.

V. Pray for us, O holy Mother of God,
R. That we may be made worthy of the promises of Christ.

Amen.

Salve, Regina, mater misericordiae; vita, dulcedo et spes nostra, salve. Ad te clamamus exsules filii Hevae. Ad te suspiramus gementes et flentes in hac lacrimarum valle. Eia ergo, advocata nostra, illos tuos misericordes oculos ad nos converte. Et Iesum, benedictum fructum ventris tui, nobis post hoc exsilium ostende. O clemens, o pia, o dulcis Virgo Maria.

V. Ora pro nobis, sancta Dei Genitrix.
R. Ut digni efficamur promissionibus Christi.

Amen.

Closing Prayer

O God, whose only begotten Son, by His life, death, and resurrection, has purchased for us the rewards of eternal salvation, grant, we beseech Thee, that while meditating on these mysteries of the most holy Rosary of the Blessed Virgin Mary, that we may both imitate what they contain and obtain what they promise, through Christ our Lord.

Amen.

Deus, cuius Unigenitus per vitam, mortem et resurrectionem suam nobis salutis aeternae praemia comparavit: concede, quaesumus; ut, haec mysteria sacratissimo beatae Mariae Virginis Rosario recolentes. et imitemur quod continent, et quod promittunt, assequamur. Per eundem Christum Dominum nostrum.

Amen.

Appetizers

• •

Margo Taylor, Kathy Loreto, & Deborah Brement

BAKED ARTICHOKES

Mrs. Rose Lombino

4 large artichokes
¼ c. Romano cheese
1 tsp. salt
¼ c. oil
1 c. bread crumbs
½ garlic clove, minced
½ tsp. pepper

Cut artichokes in halves and boil in salted water until tender. Drain. Mix bread crumbs, cheese, garlic, salt, and pepper. Add oil to the mixture.

Fill the artichoke halves and set them in a baking dish. Add ¼ cup water to the bottom of the pan.

Bake at 350° to 375° for ½ hour.

BAKED STUFFED CLAMS

Angeline Bello

1 (6 1/2 or 7 oz.) can of minced clams with juice
4 slices bread (trim crust and dice it)
1 tsp. parsley
1 tsp. oregano
½ tsp. garlic powder
½ stick oleo or ½ c. oil
¼ tsp. mustard
½ tsp. celery salt (optional)
2 Tbsp, mayonnaise
2 dashes of Worcestershire sauce
2 dashes of Tabasco sauce
1 c. dry bread crumbs
3 strips bacon
Dash of salt

Melt oleo in a 10-inch frying pan; add parsley, oregano, garlic, celery (optional), and salt. Add the diced bread and brown.

Remove from heat; add clams with juice, mayonnaise, mustard, and sauces and mix well. Add bread crumbs.Mix again.

Fill clam shells or make your own shells out of aluminum foil. Fill them and add a small strip of bacon on each and broil until bacon curls. Brown these on a cookie sheet. Make shells the size of a cherrystone clam.

Yields 30

CAPONATA

Sue Ferlo

1 can minced clams, drained
1 tsp. salt
2 c. sifted flour
1 egg, beaten
1 ½ tsp. baking powder
1 c. milk

Sift flour and baking powder; add salt. Combine egg and clams and add to flour with enough milk to make a thick batter. Drop into hot fat (360°) until golden brown.

FRIED ARTICHOKE

Mrs. Henry Baptiste

Artichokes
Bread Crumbs
1 Egg
Oil

Remove all the hard leaves from the artichoke. Cut the tip of the edible leaves in half. Cut those halves into four quarters, and cut the fuzzy middle part into quarters.

Drop leaves into boiling water; boil for 20 minutes. Remove from the stove and cool.

Now, beat eggs in one dish and add bread crumbs, grated Italian cheese, salt, and black pepper in another. Dip leaves in eggs and roll in bread crumbs.

Heat oil in a saucepan. Fry the coated leaves until golden brown.

"I've enjoyed artichokes all my life. My mother would make stuffed artichokes on Easter Sunday which were delicious. I experienced fried artichokes by my first cousin Antionette (Magliocca) Taliani. She stripped the tough leaves off the artichokes until she got to the tender leaves and heart. They were then dipped in flour, beaten egg, and rolled in breadcrumbs then fried. Mouthwatering!!" – MaryAnn Rotolo

EGGPLANT BALLS

Madeline Scerra

1 large eggplant
2 green peppers, chopped
¾ c. bread crumbs
1 tsp. paprika
2 Tbsp. olive oil
1 onion, grated
2 eggs
2 tsp. salt
1 Tbsp, cheese, grated
Flour
Tomato sauce

Pare and cut up eggplant; cover with boiling water and cook until tender. Drain and cool. Mix onion, pepper, 1 egg, ½ cup bread crumbs, salt, paprika, and cheese with eggplant. Roll into balls and dip in flour, second beaten egg, and roll in bread crumbs Fry in hot olive oil.

Serve with tomato sauce. Serves 6.

GREEN TOMATOES

Rose Rossi

1-bushel of green tomatoes, cut into slices
1 ½ lb. salt
1 bunch of celery, cut up
6 green peppers

2 qt. oil
2 qt. vinegar
1 large box of oregano
5 cloves garlic

Put tomatoes in layers; sprinkle with salt in bushel basket. Let drain overnight with a weight on the basket.

Mix together celery and peppers. Add oil, vinegar, oregano, and garlic. Stir well. Put in jars and store in the cold until ready to serve.

HOMEMADE LUPINIS

Sue Ferlo

1 lb. Lupini beans
Salt

Soak lupini for 2 or 3 days in a 14 or 16-quart kettle filled with salted water.

Drain lupinis, rinse, and place in the large kettle with water. Add ½ c. salt and boil for 1 hour or until cooked. Turn the heat off and let stand until cooled.

Drain. Place lupinis back in the same kettle and cover with water and ½ c. salt. Change water every day and add a new cup of salt for 7 days until done (sweet, not bitter). Keep lupinis in a jar filled with water and salt to taste.

HUSH PUPPIES

Lucille Barnett

4 ears of fresh corn
1 c. all-purpose flour
1 c. yellow cornmeal
1 Tbsp, baking powder
1 tsp. sugar
1 tsp. salt
1/2 c. milk
1/2 c. chopped onion
1 egg, lightly beaten
1/4 c. butter, melted

Cut corn kernels from cobs and set them aside.

Combine flour, cornmeal, baking powder, sugar, and salt. Add milk, onion, eggs, butter, and reserved corn. Stir until just blended.

Butter baking sheets. Drop tablespoonful-size mixture on baking sheets about 2 inches apart. Bake at

425° until golden, about 15 minutes. Serve warm.

(I like powdered sugar sprinkled on them.)

PRIZE ANTIPASTO

Mary Basile

½ head lettuce
1 can tuna fish, drained
1 can anchovies, drained
1 small red onion, sliced
½ c. pitted green olives
½ c. pitted black olives
¼ lb. salami, cut into thin strips
¼ lb. boiled ham, cut into thin strips
¼ lb. Provolone cheese, cubed

Arrange lettuce in bite-sized pieces on an attractive platter. Do not add salt.

Arrange other ingredients in a pleasing pattern on the lettuce.

Refrigerate until time to serve. To serve, sprinkle the antipasto generously with your favorite Italian dressing.

STUFFED ARTICHOKES

Mrs. Mary Lombino

4 large artichokes
2 Tbsp. chopped parsley
1 c. dried bread crumbs
⅓ c. grated Romano cheese
Salt, pepper, and garlic to taste
3 Tbsp. oil

Cut off stems of artichokes and about ½ inch of the top. Remove large outer leaves around the base. Spread leaves apart gently.

Combine crumbs, parsley, salt, pepper, garlic, cheese, and oil, and mix thoroughly. Place crumb mixture between artichoke leaves.

Stand artichokes straight up in a saucepan and pour water into the pan from the side. Do not pour water over the tops of the artichokes. Cover and simmer until leaves pull off easily, about ½ hour. Lift out of pan gently, and serve hot or cold.

STUFFED HOT PEPPERS

Clara Boiko

1 large jar of hot cherry peppers
1 loaf of Italian bread, unsliced
1 can anchovies
1 c. grated Italian cheese

¼ c. minced parsley
¼ c. oil
4 Tbsp, pepper juice
Salt and pepper to taste

Remove the inner part of the bread and break it into small pieces. Chop anchovies, and mix all ingredients together. Soak in oil and pepper juice. Clean out peppers and stuff with filling. Place on greased cookie sheet. Bake at 375° for 1/2 hour.

ZUCCHINI FRITTERS

Beverly Zigrino

1 ½ c. sifted flour
2 tsp. baking powder
¾ tsp. salt
1 c. milk
1 egg, beaten
1 c. finely chopped zucchini
Crisco for deep frying

In a medium bowl, stir together flour, baking powder, and salt. Combine milk, egg, and zucchini; add to dry ingredients and mix just until moistened. Drop from tablespoon into deep heated Crisco. Fry until golden, 3 to 4 minutes.

Drain on a paper towel. Makes 24 fritters.

ZUCCHINI TORTA

Mrs. Dominick Marchione

4 c. diced, raw zucchini
1 ½ c. Bisquick
½ c. grated cheese
5 eggs
½ c. fresh parsley

1 clove garlic, minced
1 green onion, chopped fine
¼ c. oil
Salt and pepper

Beat eggs; add cheese, oil, onion, garlic, parsley, Bisquick, salt, and pepper. Mix thoroughly; add zucchini.

Pour into a lightly oiled cake pan. Bake at 350° for 45 minutes or until lightly browned.

Cool; cut into strips, then into small squares.

Beverages

Pasta Cici Dinner, L to R: Gary Rice, Marilyn McGowan, Carol Brawdy, MaryAnn Rotolo, Anthony Rotolo

CRANBERRY JUICE PUNCH

Marie George

1 qt. cranberry juice
1 large can of lemon juice (frozen)
1 large can of orange juice (frozen)

1 qt. pineapple juice
4 qt. ginger ale
1 bottle gin

Mix well all juices together. Add ice cubes, gin, and ginger ale.

DANDELION WINE

Mrs. Pauline Gratch

2 qt. dandelion flowers, packed tight

Add dandelions to one gallon of boiling water. Remove from fire and let stand for 24 hours.

Squeeze the flowers out well and throw their remains away. Take the juice and bring to a heated point, remove it from the fire and add:

8 lbs. sugar.
1 more gallon of cold water
1 doz. sliced oranges
½ doz. sliced lemons
6 lbs. seedless raisins.

Let's stand in the crock for 20 days. Stir and squeeze the fruit three times a week.

After 20 days, squeeze the fruits tight and place the juice in a bag to strain to make the wine nice and clear. Then place in gallons, but do not seal until it stops working.

"When sipping on a glass of red wine on my back porch, the memory of making wine with my father comes to mind. It's something I will never forget. Fall is the time to make wine, and every year at that time you could smell the empty grape boxes throughout East Rome. We never washed the grape; the skin has natural yeast so you don't want to wash it away. We would grind the grapes and remove the vines, Then, we put the juice/grape mixture into a whiskey barrel to let it ferment for several days until it had the correct sugar content. After that, we siphoned the wine from the barrel and pressed the remaining grape. Finally, we would install the wine into another barrel and seal it. Thank you, Dad, for all the lessons and experiences you shared with me."
– Carmine Stagliano

EGG NOG

Delcie Castro

4 eggs
¼ c. sugar
1 qt. cold milk
1 ½ tsp. vanilla
¼ tsp. salt
Nutmeg to your liking

Beat 3 whole eggs and 1 yolk until light in color. Add 3 ½ tablespoons of sugar and beat well. Stir in milk, vanilla, and salt.

Beat the remaining egg white and add the remaining sugar and nutmeg to the mixture.

FRUITED PUNCH (for large quantities)

Mrs. Sara Messineo

4 qt. orange juice(20 to 30 fresh oranges, or 5-6 oz. of frozen, orange juice, and 3 qt. water)
2 qt. lemon juice (30 to 25 fresh lemons, or 11 cans of frozen lemon juice)
1 qt. pineapple juice
1 qt. strawberry, red raspberry or cranberry juice
1 ½ qt. Tea (6 Tbsp. tea and 7 c. boiling water)
5 c. sugar (if using fresh fruit)
1 c. water
4 qt. ginger ale
8 qt. cracked ice

Combine the juices with the tea infusion. Combine the sugar (if used) and water; boil for five minutes. Cool, and add to the fruit juices. Chill.

Add the ginger ale and ice just before serving. Lime, pineapple, or orange slices may be added to the punch. Just before serving float scoops of ice on top of the fruited punch in a large punch bowl. Yields 3 ½ gallons.

ORANGE JULIUS

Mary F. Lanzi

½ (6 oz. can) orange juice	¼ c. sugar	Put all ingredients through a blender
½ c. milk	½ tsp. vanilla	for 30 seconds and serve.
½ c. water	5 or 6 ice cubes	

PINEAPPLE MINT JULEP

Mrs. Bambina Schillaci

6 sprigs fresh mint	3 c. unsweetened pineapple juice
¾ c. sugar	3 c. ginger ale
¾ c. lemon juice	

Wash the mint leaves, bruise them with a spoon, and cover them with sugar. Add lemon juice. Let stand for about 15 minutes.

Add pineapple juice, pour over ice in a pitcher or tall glass, add ginger ale.

Garnish with springs of mint. Makes about 8 servings.

St. Anne's Night *1958*
Church of St. John the Baptist
200 East Dominick St.

Monday, February 3rd — 6:00 P.M. and 7:30 P.M.
SERVICES IN HONOR OF GOOD SAINT ANNE
Candlelight Procession and Veneration of St. Anne's Relic
Conducted as at St. Anne de Beaupre' in Canada
by
Rev. Eugene Lefebvre, CSSR
All Cordially Invited to Attend

Breads, Rolls & Muffins

· ·

JUNE 15, 1956

CHURCH GROUPS INSTALLATION—Leaders of the seven organizations of St. John the Baptist Church were installed last night at a banquet at Club Martin. From the left, seated, are Mrs. Silvo R. Barone, Ladies Auxiliary prefect; Mrs. Jerry Z. Corigliano, Mother of Christ Sodality prefect; the Rev. Victor F. Ciciarelli, pastor, and Mrs. Michael Cangi, Congregation of Mary prefect. Standing, from left, Michael Cangi, Usher Society president; Mrs. Vincent D. Petrucci, Ave Maria Sodality prefect; Miss Jean Rosati, Sodality of Our Lady prefect and Anthony J. Marullo, Holy Name Society president.

BREADS

BREAD DOUGH

Mary F. Lanzi

1 large yeast
3 c. warm water
1 tsp. salt
Flour (as much as it takes)

Put about 6 cups of flour in a bowl and make a well. Dissolve yeast in 1/2 cup of warm water. Pour into the well with the remaining 2 ½ cups of water and salt and beat with a mixer until it won't take it. Finish kneading dough on a floured board until smooth and elastic.

Oil a large bowl and place the dough inside until it rises double in size. Shape into loaves, and let rise for another hour.

Bake at 400° for about 25 minutes or until done.

This dough may also be used for sausage bread or pizza.

BROWN BREAD

Katherine Kane

½ c. brown sugar
1 Tbsp melted lard
½ c. molasses
1 c. sweet milk
1 c. sour milk
2 c. ground flour
1 c. white flour

1 tsp. baking powder
1 tsp. baking soda
¼ c. boiling water
½ tsp. salt
½ c. raisins

Blend sugar and melted lard. Add molasses and milk.

Sift flour, baking powder, soda, and salt; mix in with the first mixture. Add raisins.

Bake at 350° for 1 hour.

Sr. Mary Josita, Sr. Joan Germain, Sr. Linda Jean Marie, & Mary K Swerediuk

CHERRY (MARASCHINO) LOAF

....

Marie George

1 c. melted Crisco
1 c. sugar
3 eggs
1 tsp. anise flavoring
1 (10 oz.) bottle of maraschino
cherries and juice, cut up

1 tsp. baking powder
1 to 6 c. flour
1 c. nutmeats

Mix all ingredients together until the mixture begins to leave the sides of the bowl. The dough should be soft and not too hard.

Form into loaves and place on a greased cookie sheet. Bake at 350" for 15 to 20 minutes. Make butter icing and spread lightly over the loaves. Slice before serving.

Makes 4 to 6 loaves.

"As many of you know, I make my own bread. Bringing back the memory of my mother making hers. But she proofed her's overnight." - Father Joseph Sestito

DATE NUT BREAD

....

Mrs. Mary Fusco

1 lb. cut-up dates
1 tsp. baking soda
2 c. boiling water
1 c. sugar
1 heaping Tbsp. butter
2 eggs
3 ½ c. flour

2 tsp. baking powder
Pinch of salt
1 c. chopped nuts

Mix dates with baking soda and water. Let sit. Add sugar, eggs, flour, baking powder, salt, and nuts.

Bake at 375° for 30 minutes.

This recipe makes 2 loaves of bread.

"My mom, Marie, would probably kill me for telling this story of a memory she shared with me. Well, I'm going to tell you anyway. My mom told me that my grandmother used to make bread from scratch. My grandfather would help my grandmother with the preparations by adding flour as she kneaded the bread. When it was ready to be baked, my grandmother would slide it into her oven. My mom said how delicious it smelled and that she could hardly wait to eat it.

"When my mom got married and as a new bride, she wanted to surprise my dad with her own homemade bread. She made it from scratch as well and when it was time to bake it, she shoved it into the oven just the way my grandmother did. Now, the type of oven my dad bought for my mom was a newer model compared to what my grandmother had used. When it came time for my mother to check to see if the bread was done baking she had quite the surprise. Lo and behold, when my mom opened the oven door, the bread was all over the oven grates. It was like an I Love Lucy episode. She had no idea she could not just slide the bread in that type of oven, but instead, she needed to put the bread in a bread pan before putting it into the oven. When my mother told my father what had happened, my father just kept silent."

- Crystal D'Ambrosi

DATE NUT BREAD
....
Mary F. Lanzi

1 lb. dates
2 c. boiling water
1 tsp. baking soda

Add baking soda and boiling water to dates. Let stand until cool.

Add:
1 scant c. sugar
1 heaping Tbsp. butter
2 eggs, well beaten
3 1/2 c. flour
2 tsp. baking powder
Pinch of salt
3/4 c. nutmeats

Bake for 30 minutes in a 375° oven.

EASTER BREAD
....
Mrs. Rosario Damar

"With an egg on it or without? That was a major decision for us as kids. Then we had to decide whether to braid the bread or make it round. Each family has a different way of making and decorating their traditional Easter bread."
– Patti Martinelli

1 ¼ c. milk, lukewarm
1 ½ c. sugar
1 tsp. salt
1 packaged dry yeast
1 whole egg
2 egg yolks
1 teaspoon lemon for a nice flavor
⅓ c. soft butter
6 c. flour

Mix milk, sugar, and salt. Stir in the yeast, which has been dissolved as directed. Then stir in the eggs, flavoring, and soft butter.

Mix in flour and knead until the dough is velvety and smooth. Place on a floured board, cover, and let stand for 10 minutes to tighten up. Then knead a little and "let stand until it doubles in size; about two hours.

Punch dough down and let stand for 30 minutes then shape it into round loaves or nests for boiled eggs. Place on a cookie sheet and let rise for about 30 minutes.

Heat oven to 375° and bake for 30 or 40 minutes.

Icing:
¾ c. confectionery sugar
1 Tbsp. warm milk
1 teaspoon lemon juice

Spread icing over bread when cooled.

EASTER SWEET BREAD

Mary F. Lanzi

12 eggs
2 c. sugar
2 sticks butter
1 large pkg. yeast
Rind and juice of 2 oranges
3 Tbsp. lemon extract
3 Tbsp. anise seed
1 ½ c. warm water
1 c. warm milk
About 5 lb. flour

Beat eggs with mixer; add sugar, melted oleo, flavorings and yeast dissolved in 1/2 cup warm water. Add warm milk, remaining water and flour - use a mixer until it won't take it. Finish kneading it on floured board, then let the dough rise in an oiled bowl.

Cover and let rise until double. Shape into loaves and let rise for 2 hours. When ready for baking, brush with beaten egg, and make slits on top of the bread with a razor blade or sharp knife.

Bake at 325° for 25 minutes or until done.

IRISH BROWN BREAD

Jennie Sanzone

2 c. sugar
2 c. water
1 (15 oz.) package seedless raisins
½ c. butter or margarine
1 tsp. baking soda
1 c. flour, spooned into cup
1 tsp. each nutmeg and cinnamon
½ tsp. cloves

Blend sugar and water; cook for 3 minutes or until boiling. Add raisins. Simmer for 3 minutes or until the raisins are tender. Remove from heat; add butter; let stand 15 minutes or until cool.

Add baking soda. Mix flour and spices together. Blend with raisin mixture. Pour into a buttered, floured pan (9 x 5 x 23/4 inches).

Bake at 350° for 1 hour or until the knife inserted comes out clean.

OATMEAL BREAD

Mrs. Lewell E. Isom

"This homemade oatmeal bread makes a superb sandwich and stays soft for several days. Even then, it's excellent for toast and it freezes well, so it's a great make-ahead recipe. It's also a perfect Sunday baking project with your family. You then can enjoy homemade bread with your Sunday macaroni or meatball sandwiches."
– MaryAnn Rotolo

1 ½ c. boiling water
2 tsp. salt
1 Tbsp. shortening
1 c. uncooked rolled oats
2 yeast cakes, dissolved in ¾ c. lukewarm water
¼ c. molasses
¼ c. brown sugar
1 c. flour

Combined first four ingredients. Let's stand for ½ an hour until lukewarm.

Add dissolved yeast cakes, molasses, brown sugar, and one cup of flour; beat until smooth. Into this rolled oats mixture, sift 4 cups of flour. Mix well and turn out on floured board; knead until smooth.

Cut dough into two pieces, flatten, and cover for ½ an hour.

Place loaves in greased pans and let rise until double in bulk. Then bake at 375° for about 45 minutes.

PUMPKIN BREAD

Mary F. Lanzi

3 c. sugar
1 c. oil
4 eggs
1 (No. 2) can pumpkin (2 c.)
1 ¼ tsp. salt
1 tsp. nutmeg

1 tsp. cinnamon
1 tsp. cloves
½ tsp. baking powder
2 tsp. baking soda
3 ⅓ c. flour

Bake at 325° 1 ½ hours. Makes 2 loaves

QUICK NUT BREAD

Mrs. Virginia Pisao

2-4 two c. sifted flour
4 level tsp. baking powder
1 tsp. salt
2 c. chopped walnuts
¾ to 1 c. sugar
2 eggs
1 ½ milk
2 Tbsp. melted butter

Sift flour, baking powder, and salt; add sugar and walnuts, and mix well.

In a small bowl, beat the eggs lightly, add the milk mix, and pour into the dry ingredients. Add melted butter and stir till smooth pour into two well-greased loaf pans lined with wax paper.

Bake at 350° for one hour. Cool and store.

If dates are desired, use ½ c. dates and ½ c. nuts.

ZUCCHINI BREAD

Antoinette Guaspari

1 c. Crisco oil
1 c. flour
1 egg
1 c. sugar
2 c. peeled and chopped fine zucchini
3 tsp. vanilla
½ c. chopped nuts
1 tsp. baking soda
¼ tsp. baking powder
3 tsp. cinnamon
1 c. chocolate chips

Beat eggs until fluffy; add oil, sugar, and vanilla, and beat.

Add zucchini and dry ingredients a little at a time. When mixed well, add nuts and chocolate chips.

Grease and flour loaf pan or coffee cans. Bake at 350° for 50 to 60 minutes.

MUFFINS

BRAN MUFFINS

Mary F. Lanzi

2 c. raw bran
1 ½ c. unbleached flour
1 ½ tsp. salt
½ c. brown sugar, packed
1 tsp. baking soda

1 ½ c. milk or buttermilk
1 egg
½ c. vegetable oil

Mix dry ingredients. Make a well in the center of the dry mixture and pour liquids into it. Mix until all dry ingredients are incorporated.

Bake at 450° for 20 minutes.

ZUCCHINI MUFFINS

Concetta Griffo

2 c. flour
1¼ c. sugar
2 tsp. cinnamon
¼ tsp. salt
2 tsp. baking soda

Put these ingredients in a large bowl:
1 c. grated carrots
1 c. grated zucchini
½ c. raisins
½ c. chopped nutmeats
1 apple, grated

Beat 3 eggs with 1 cup salad oil. Add 2 teaspoons vanilla. Combine with above and add to ingredients in large bowl. Fill muffin tins to top. Bake at 350° for 20 minutes.

Confirmation, April 1961

ROLLS

COTTAGE CHEESE ROLLS

Josephine Taverna

1 c. cottage cheese
½ lb. butter or margarine
2 c. flour
½ tsp. vvanilla
Brown sugar
Nuts of choice

Cream the cottage cheese and butter. Add flour and vanilla. Chill the mixture for a few hours.

Divide dough in half on a floured board. Roll into two circles about ⅛ inch thick. Spread melted butter over the dough and sprinkle with brown sugar and nuts. Then, cut circles into 16 wedge-shaped slices and roll them into rolls, starting with the wider side. Repeat the procedure with the remaining dough.

Place on greased cookie sheet. Bake at 400° for 20 to 25 minutes.

Roll in powdered sugar while they are still warm.

ROLLS

Mrs. Louis Coluccio

1 Tbsp, lard or 2 Tbsp. Spry, melted
1 c. milk
1 c. water
1 tsp. salt
½ c. sugar
2 eggs, well beaten
1 oz. yeast
6 c. flour

Dissolve yeast with 1/2 cup water.

Dissolve sugar and salt with the milk, water, and melted shortening. Add flour and knead for 20 minutes. Cover the dough with a wet cloth and let it rise over a pan of warm water for 1 hour.

Knead the dough for a few more minutes. Then shape it into rolls. Let these rise another hour.

When the dough has doubled in size, place it in the oven at 425° for 20 minutes. Remove the rolls and brush with Spry while they're still hot.

Soups
& Salads

SACRIFICE TRIP FOR CHURCH—The Misses Angela M. De Mare, Teresa A. De Costy and Doreen M. Sestito, members of the Teen-Age Sodality, could have gone to the Summer School of Catholic Action at Fordham University with expenses paid. But they believed the new church planned for St. John the Baptist parish is more important. Consequently they turned over their paid expenses to the pastor, the Rev. Victor F. Ciciarelli, shown receiving a check for $100 from Miss De Mare, vice-prefect of the Sodality. Others, from the left, are Miss Carmella A. Mungari, secretary; Miss De Costy, Miss Palma M. Natale, prefect, and Miss Sestito, treasurer.

August - 1953

SOUPS

● ●

BARLEY SOUP

Louise Mascicki

2 to 3 lb. soup shank or short ribs
6 qt. water
3 carrots, sliced
½ onion, chopped
1 can tomatoes
3 stalks of celery, plus leaves
½ c. barley
Season-All, pepper, parsley

Boil shanks or ribs in water for 20 minutes on medium heat. Skim off the top. Add vegetables. Season to taste. Simmer for 3 1/2 hours. Put tomatoes in a blender and add to soup. Simmer another 1/2 hour; add barley, and simmer another hour.

BROWN RICE AND LENTIL SOUP

Dolly Flaver

1½ c. diced carrots
1 c. chopped onion
½ c. chopped celery
3 cloves garlic, chopped
8 c. chicken or vegetable stock
1 (14-oz.) can tomatoes, coarsely chopped
1½ c. lentils
1½ tsp. dried basil

1½ tsp. dried thyme
1½ tsp. dried oregano
½ tsp. dried hot red pepper flakes, optional
2 bay leaves
Salt and pepper to taste
½ c. chopped parsley
1 c. uncooked brown rice

In a large kettle, combine the vegetable stock, tomatoes, lentils, rice, and herbs except for the parsley. Bring to a boil and simmer, stirring occasionally, for about 35 minutes. Season with salt and pepper and remove the bay leaves. Add the parsley and serve.

Note: Lentils do not need to be soaked before cooking.

CHICKEN SOUP

Mary F. Lanzi

½ stewing chicken
2 to 3 stalks of celery with leaves
1 to 4 carrots, sliced
Salt and pepper to taste

Wash chicken in salted water. Place chicken in a 6-quart pot and cover with water. Bring to a boil and skim off the top.

Add celery leaves, salt, and pepper to taste and simmer for about 1 hour. Add diced-up celery and sliced carrots and continue to simmer until the chicken is cooked.

Remove chicken from the soup and cut or shred it into little pieces and return to the pot of soup.

Let soup cool and refrigerate. Next day remove the chicken fat that will rise to the top.

CHICKEN SOUP WITH GREENS

Mary F. Lanzi

1 or 2 heads of endive
½ lb. hamburger
2 to 3 eggs

Wash and cut up endive. Cook in boiling water until done. Drain and squeeze dry. Cut into smaller pieces. Meanwhile, make meatballs with the hamburger.

Put chicken soup into a 3-quart pot and bring to a boil. When the soup boils, make little tiny meatballs and drop the raw meatballs into the soup. When the meatballs rise to the top they are done, then you must add the endive and let that cook for 15 to 20 minutes.

Lastly, add 2 to 3 beaten eggs to which you have added a little salt and some Parmesan cheese and mix it through the soup.

ITALIAN VEGETABLE BEEF SOUP

Mrs. Angeline Volpe

2 lb. soup meat
4 fresh carrots
2 stalks celery
small celery leaves
1 onion
2 tomatoes
1 potato
Pinch of salt

Run some fresh water on the soup meat before using it. Drain it.

Put about 4 quarts of water, along with a pinch of salt and the soup meat into a 6 quart pan. Let it boil until scum forms on top. Gradually remove all of the scum as it forms.

In the meantime, prepare your vegetables by peeling, washing, and shredding them. You can strain the tomatoes if you want.

When there isn't any more scum, add all the vegetables to the water solution. Let this cook until everything is cooked. When the meat is cooked, you can take it out and shred it, then you will put it in a soup again and let it simmer for a while.

Pastina can also be added.

Serves about 4 to 6 people.

LENTIL SOUP WITH BABY MEATBALLS

Rosalie Henry

"This is a fabulous, hearty meal, and so easy to make. Try ladling this soup over white rice and top with grated Romano cheese. It's perfect for a cold winter day." – MaryAnn Rotolo

1 pkg. lentils
¾ lb. hamburger
2 stalks celery, cut up
1 onion, chopped
2 carrots, chopped fine
1 small can Hunt's tomato sauce

Wash lentils and put them in a Dutch oven. Fill with water and add celery, onion, carrots, and sauce. Let boil for about 5 minutes. Mix hamburger with bread crumbs, salt, pepper, and 2 eggs. Make meatballs the size of a dime and drop them into the soup mixture. Let cook until the meatballs are done.

Make rice according to the directions and add to the soup mixture.

Serves 8 people.

MEDITERRANEAN MINESTRONE

A Friend

"This soup is a wonderful hearty warm dish to serve on a cold winter day, along with focaccia bread. MMM Good!" – MaryAnn Rotolo

2 lb. beef soup bones
3 lb. shin beef, sliced
4 qt. water
1 (28 oz.) can of tomatoes in puree or juice, undrained
1 (15 oz.) can of tomato sauce
2 medium onions, quartered
¼ c. chopped parsley
2 Tbsp. salt
½ tsp. ground black pepper
2 tsp. basil leaves, crushed
1 (10 oz.) pkg. frozen peas
¼ tsp. garlic powder
2 bay leaves
2 c. sliced carrots
2 c. sliced celery
4 c. uncooked shell macaroni
2 pkg. (9 oz. each) frozen Italian green beans
1 (1 lb. or 20 oz.) can of white or red kidney beans, undrained
Parmesan cheese
Italian bread

Place soup bones and shin beef in a large 8 to 10-quart soup kettle, add water. Bring to boil; skim the surface of the liquid if desired. Add tomatoes, tomato sauce, onions, parsley, salt, basil, pepper, garlic powder, and bay leaves. Bring to boil again; reduce heat; cover and simmer for 1 1/2 hours. Add carrots and celery; cover and simmer 1/2 hour longer, or until meat is fork tender. Remove meat and bones for soup. Discard bones and fat. Cut meat into bite-size pieces and return to soup. Heat soup to boiling. Add uncooked macaroni, green beans, and peas. Simmer, covered, about 15 to 20 minutes longer, or until macaroni is tender. Stir occasionally. Stir in kidney beans; heat until soup is bubbling. Serve in large, deep soup bowls. Pass grated cheese and Italian bread.

Makes about 6 quarts.

MY MINESTRONE SOUP
....
Amy Breton

1/4 lb. small white beans
(navy or pea)
3 Tbsp. oil
2 onions, sliced
2 cloves garlic, crushed
2 to 3 slices bacon
4 tomatoes, chopped
1 small glass red wine
1 tsp. marjoram
1/2 tsp. thyme
2 carrots, cubed

1 potato, cubed
1 Tbsp. chopped parsley
Salt and pepper to taste
1 small turnip, cubed (optional)
1 to 2 stalks of celery, chopped
1/2 small cabbage, shredded
1/2 c. small pasta (little shells, stars, or spaghetti,
cut into 1-inch pieces)
12 to 14 tiny meatballs, browned (optional)*
Grated Parmesan cheese

Soak beans overnight. Heat oil in a large saucepan; add onion, garlic, and bacon and saute for a few minutes. Some people like to add small tiny browned meatballs at this time. Add tomatoes, wine, and beans. Add 3 pints of water, marjoram, and thyme and simmer for about 2 hours, covered. Add carrots; cook for 10 minutes. Add potatoes and turnips. Cook a few minutes longer and then add celery, cabbage, and pasta. Cook until pasta and all vegetables are tender, then add chopped parsley, salt, and pepper and stir in 2 to 3 tablespoons of grated Parmesan cheese.

* Serve with extra Parmesan cheese sprinkled over individual bowls of minestrone.

*Variation: Some Italians like to add 1/2 cup of pre-cooked rice to the above ingredients, just before serving.

MINESTRONE SOUP
....
Mrs. Helen Natale

1 medium head of cabbage
1 medium head of Savoy cabbage
1 pkg. spinach or other greens like escarole, endive, or dandelion greens (according to your to own taste)
1 lb. soup meat
1 lb. smoked ham
One stick of pepperoni sausage
Salt and pepper to taste

Wash and cook the greens. After the greens are cooked, remove them and let them drain. Then add water to soup meat, ham, and pepperoni to make broth. When meat is cooked, remove it from the broth and crumble it into small pieces. Cut the greens into small pieces, combine meat and greens, and place them into the broth. Let simmer for 10 or 15 minutes.

When serving sprinkle Italian grated cheese on top.

Serves 8

MINESTRONE

....

Mrs. Lena Vittorello

1 small cabbage, shredded
1 ½ lb. green beans, small pieces
I celery stalk, diced
2 carrots, diced
2 medium potatoes, diced
1 c. canned tomatoes
¾ c. peas

Mix all ingredients together and add to three quarts of boiling, salted water. Boil for 15 minutes, then add pesto:

¼ lb. fat-back, chopped very fine
½ c. fresh or dry basil
¾ c. grated cheese
2 large garlic cloves
½ c. fresh or dry parsley
2 Tbsp. olive oil.

Combine the above ingredients and mix to form a paste. Add paste to the soup and bring to a boil. Let simmer for about 2 hours, and then remove from heat.

In a separate pan, cook ½ lb. broken spaghetti in salted water. When cooked, drain and add to vegetable mixture.

More grated cheese may be added when served.

Note: Lentils do not need to be soaked before cooking.

SAVORY CABBAGE WITH BEANS

....

Theresa DiStefano

3 lb. head savory cabbage
1 (16 oz.) can white or red kidney beans
2 cloves garlic
¼ c. oil
Pinch of salt
Pinch of red pepper

Cut and wash cabbage. Drain. Cook in boiling water until tender. Drain again. In covered saucepan, mince garlic and oil, add cabbage. Simmer slowly for ½ hour. Add the kidney beans (juice and all). Add the salt and pepper to taste.

Cover and cook for an additional half-hour.

SALADS

• •

HAPPY HOUR SALAD

Luigina Curcio

1 c. sour cream (commercial)
1 c. crushed pineapple, drained
1 c. coconut
1 c. miniature marshmallows
1 c. Mandarin oranges, drained

Mix all together except for the oranges, then fold the oranges in last. Chill until ready to eat.

HOT GERMAN POTATO SALAD

Miss Catherine Diodato

2 lb. sliced, boiled potatoes
6 slices bacon
¾ c. chopped onion
2 Tbsp. flour
2 Tbsp. sugar
2 tsp. salt
½ tsp. celery seed
Dash pepper
⅓ c. vinegar
¾ c. water

In large skillet, fry bacon until crisp. Remove and drain. Crumble when cool. Cook and stir onion in bacon drippings until tender. Stir in flour, sugar, salt, celery seed and pepper. Cook over low heat, stirring until bubbly. Remove from heat and stir in water and vinegar. Heat to boiling, stirring constantly. Boil and stir 1 minute. Carefully stir crumbled bacon and sliced potatoes into hot mixture. Heat thoroughly, stirring lightly to coat all potato slices. Serves 5 or 6.

INSALATA BACCALA (SALT COD FISH SALAD)

Dianna (Daniello) Wakefield

1 lb. salt cod fish
½ tsp. pepper
½ c. olive oil
2 cloves minced garlic
Juice of 1 lemon
½ c. sliced olives
2 T. red wine vinegar
1 T. fresh parsley, chopped

Soak in cold water 2 days prior to preparation. Change water frequently. Rinse cod fish in cold water several times. In a large skillet add cod fish and cover with water. Heat over a medium heat until fish starts to flake. Drain water and remove from pan. Chop fish into bite-size pieces. In a separate bowl combine olive oil, juice of 1 lemon, vinegar, garlic, pepper, sliced olives and parsley to marinate. In a large dish, place chopped cod fish; spread marinated mixture over fish and chill.

ITALIAN POTATO SALAD

Grace Bottini

8 potatoes
1 medium chopped onion
3 stalks chopped celery
1 c. chopped pole beans
Olive oil

1 tsp. salt
½ tsp. pepper
½ tsp. garlic powder
1 tsp. oregano

Boil potatoes, peel and cut into small chunks. Add chopped onion, celery, pole beans, and above seasonings. Add oil to moisten potatoes.

PICKLED GARDEN SALAD

Mrs. John Parker

1 head cauliflower, cut in pieces
6 carrots, pared and cut in pieces
6 celery stalks, cut in pieces
2 green peppers, cut in strips
1 jar green olives
3 Tbsp. sugar
¾ c. wine vinegar

1/2 c. salad oil
1 tsp. oregano leaves
1 tsp. salt
½ tsp. pepper
¼ c. water

Combine all ingredients in a large skillet. Bring to a boil, stirring occasionally. Simmer, covered, 8 minutes. Cool, then refrigerate.

THREE BEAN SALAD

Sue Rossi

1 can kidney beans
1 can yellow beans
1 can green beans
1 can chick peas
½ tsp. dry mustard
½ tsp. basil
½ tsp. oregano
2 Tbsp. parsley

Mix:
4 Tbsp, sugar
¼ c. vinegar
1 tsp. Salt
1 medium onion
½ c. oil

Mix and refrigerate overnight.

REPUBLICAN LIME SALAD

Eleanor Ferlo

"Easy to make and is always a hit. Go ahead and try this lime Jello salad on a hot summer day. It's delicious and refreshing!" – MaryAnn Rotolo

2 (3 oz.) pkg. lime Jello
2 c. boiling water
1 c. evaporated milk
1 c. mayonnaise
2 c. crushed pineapple, drained
½ c. walnuts
2 c. cottage cheese
1 tsp. salt

Dissolve gelatin in boiling water; add milk and mayonnaise; beat well. Add all other ingredients. Stir in thoroughly. Pour in 12 x 9 inch pan and chill until firm.

STRAWBERRY SOUR CREAM SALAD

Mary Basile

2 pkg. strawberry gelatin
2 (16 oz.) pkg. Frozen strawberries or raspberries
1 large can crushed pineapple, well-drained
1 c. chopped nuts
1 pt. sour cream
2 mashed bananas

Add 2 cups of hot water to gelatin to dissolve. Add bananas, nuts, strawberries and pineapple. Mix together. Put half the mixture in a serving bowl and chill. Leave other half at room temperature so it will not set. When the first part is set, spread the sour cream on top and add the remaining mixture. Chill.

Entrees

....

FINISHING TOUCHES — Joseph D. Summa, left, and Henry J. Fiaschetti put the final touches on one of the booths for the three-day festival being sponsored by the Building Fund Committee of St. John the Baptist Church. The festival, proceeds of which will go to the church building fund, will be held Friday, Saturday and Sunday on E. Dominick St., between Bouck St. and the Mohawk River bridge.

BEEF

AMAZING MEATLOAF

Annette Marullo

"My Mom, Josephine Marullo, made this for me every year on my birthday. I am so happy I remembered this dish so I can now make it for my loved ones."

Prepare the meatloaf mixture as you would a meatball. Roll flat on wax paper. Top with sauteed spinach and shredded cheddar cheese. Roll carefully and bake at 350 degrees for approximately 45 minutes. Top with a small can of sauce and let bake again until slightly crusty on top.

BISTECCA ALLA SICILIANA (SICILIAN STEAK)

Veda (Rotolo) Donnelly

4 pieces of steak of your choice
3 T. grated Parmesan cheese
2 cloves garlic, crushed
1 c. (110 g.) bread crumbs
½ c. (125 ml.) olive oil
Salt and pepper

Mix together the garlic and the oil. Dip steaks in the mixture. Combine the grated cheese, bread crumbs and salt and pepper. Coat steaks with this mixture. Cook steaks under a hot broiler, turning once.

Serves 4.

DUTCH MEAT LOAF

Madeline Scerra

1 ½ lb. ground beef
½ can tomato sauce
1 egg, beaten
4 Tbsp. minced onion
1 c. bread crumbs
¼ tsp. dry mustard
1 ½ tsp. salt
½ tsp. sage
¼ tsp. pepper

Mix into loaf. Place in shallow pan. Start baking in moderate oven at 350°.

Mix:
½ can tomato sauce
1 Tbsp. vinegar
½ c. cold water
1 Tbsp. brown sugar
1 Tbsp. prepared mustard

Pour over meat loaf. Bake 1 hour or more. Baste once or twice during baking. When serving, put 1 tablespoon on top of each serving.

GOTABKI (CABBAGE ROLLS)

Ted Buczek

1 lb. Ground Beef: (I use 85%)
½ lb. Ground Pork.
(Optional, I don't use pork)
½ cup Rice. (Optional, I use 1 cup rice for each 1b. of ground beef)
1 egg. (Optional I don't use an egg)
1 large onion, Chopped fine.
Salt and pepper to taste.
1 head of cabbage about 4 - to 5 lb.
2 T butter.

Remove core from whole head of cabbage with a sharp knife. Scald the cabbage in boiling water. Remove the leaves as they become flexible easily to roll. Don't over steam because they will cook further as you cook the cabbage rolls. I prefer Minute Rice, 1 cup of water for each cup of rice. Boil water and salt to taste, pour in the rice, let set until water is absorbed into the rice. (Optional, you can use rice of your choice.) Optional, I cut the bacon in ¼ in pieces and fry in a frying pan til almost done. I then pour out the bacon grease and replace with ¼ cup of olive oil or whatever you like. If you want, use the bacon grease. Saute the onions in with the bacon, just enough for mellowness. Take and pour the bacon and onions into the rice, mixing thoroughly to flavor throughout. Add the ground beef into the rice mixture, again salt and pepper to taste, (usually I will sample the rice mixture for taste) mix well.

Take each cabbage leaf spread out on the table (optional, I would cut the heaved cabbage core out, to make rolling easier, just the back side, not into the leaf.) Fill each leaf with the beef mixture, larger leaf more filling, smaller less, keep the core side toward you, first roll away make one roll tuck the edges in and continue to roll to complete the roll. Stack each into a cooking pan, I also stagger each row so they will cook evenly. (Optional: Some chefs will place the uncooked bacon on top of the rolled cabbage prior and during cooking.) I use tomato soup for cooking, some use tomato puree, use whatever you want. Be careful when cooking, you can burn the cabbage leaves easily. Burnt cabbage leaves don't taste good, the taste will go throughout your pan, you will ruin your dinner. Start on medium heat, as it starts boiling turn down to low heat enough heat to keep it boiling and cook usually til cabbage is tender. This recipe may sound difficult or time consuming, but it's really not. I make 40 or 50 for my family in less than an hour. Enjoy!

"My Grandma Natalie fried fresh meatballs every Sunday morning after church. We sampled a few, drank coffee, listened to the Italian (or Polish) hour on the radio, and ate Italian pastries from the pastry truck that drove by every Sunday morning." - Sharon Natalie Abramski

FATHER PAUL'S MEATBALLS

Father Paul Angelicchio

1 1b. ground beef
¼ lb. ground pork
2 cloves minced fresh garlic
salt and pepepr to taste
¼ c. fresh Romano cheese
½ c. Italian bread crumbs
2 eggs
¼ c. tomato sauce
½ c. Ritz crackers, crushed

Mix all together. Roll into round balls.
Fry until done, add to your favorite sauce and enjoy.

HUNGARIAN GOULASH

Felicia Cambopiano

1 lb. beef, cubed
2 onions, chopped
3 c. water
2 tsp. dry mustard
3 tsp. Worcestershire sauce
½ c. ketchup

1 tsp. brown sugar
3 Tbsp. vinegar
½ tsp. allspice
Salt and pepper to taste

Brown the beef, then add water and remaining ingredients. Simmer for 2 hours. Later thicken with flour and water. Cook egg noodles (medium wide), drain them, fry with butter to brown, and serve in individual dishes with Hungarian Goulash over the noodles. Bon Appetit.

MEATLOAF WITH MASHED POTATO COVERING

Millie Rauilli

1 lb. ground veal
1 ½ lb. ground pork
¾ lb. ground beef
½ powdered sage
1 ½ tsp. salt
1 tsp. pepper
¼ c. chopped onion
¾ c. ketchup
½ c. breadcrumbs or oatmeal
2 eggs, slightly beaten
1 c. liquid milk or tomato juice
1 c. thinly sliced carrots
2 ½ c. dry mashed potatoes

Combine all ingredients except potatoes, ketchup, and flour. Reserve one tablespoon of beaten egg for brushing potato frosting. Mix the remaining ingredients well and pack in a medium-sized baking pan.

Bake at 350° for 1 ½ hour.

Make the sauce by thickening the liquid from the loaf. Using the meat drippings, stir in 2 Tbsp. flour, and add cold water to every cup of liquid. Stir in ketchup.

Unmold meatloaf on a baking sheet and frost it with mashed potatoes. Brush with beaten egg and brown in a very hot oven 450°.

PEPPER STEAK

Phyllis DeMartini

1 lb. round steak (cut in 1/4 inch strips)
8 green peppers, sliced
3 medium onions, sliced
4 Tbsp. flour
2 c. water
2 c. ketchup
1 ¾ c. soy sauce

Brown steak in oil, just covering bottom of large skillet. Remove meat from pan. Drain oil.

In bowl, mix together flour, water, ketchup, and soy sauce. Add to skillet. Add meat, onions, and peppers. Simmer and cover for 2 hours or until meat is tender. Stir occasionally.

Delicious with garlic bread.

PIZZIOLA (Italian Swiss Steak)

Mrs. Rose Swerediuk

½ canned tomatoes
1 lb. round steak
1 clove garlic, chopped
1 tsp. oregano, chopped
1 tsp. parsley, chopped
salt and pepper to taste

Cover the bottom of the skillet generously with cooking oil. Cut round steak into small pieces and arrange in a skillet. Sprinkle chopped garlic, parsley, oregano, and salt and pepper on top of the round steak. Then cover the steaks with tomatoes and let simmer in a covered skillet for approximately 35 minutes.

Serves 4 people. More tomatoes may be used if desired.

SAUSAGE AND MEATBALL CACCIATORE

Bertha Domenico

1 lb. Italian sausage
½ lb. ground chuck
8 peppers
1 clove garlic
3 small onions (whole)
2 stalks celery
1 (8 oz.) can mushrooms
1 large can Italian tomatoes
Salt and pepper

Cut sausage in 1 inch pieces. Make small meatballs. Fry in Dutch oven until brown; remove excess grease. Add garlic, chopped fine and tomatoes. Simmer 1 1/2 hours. Add cut peppers, celery, onions, mushrooms. Cook 30 minutes longer. Serve and sprinkle with Italian grated cheese.

STEAMED STRING BEANS WITH BEEF

Rosalie Henry

2 thick chuck steaks, cut up
½ c. grated cheese in serving pieces
1 tsp. salt
2 lb. string beans
1 tsp. pepper
1 can crushed tomatoes

Brown chuck steaks in a frying pan. Set aside.

In a roaster, put half of the string beans. On top of the string beans, put half of the chuck steaks. Put half of the tomatoes on top and sprinkle half of the cheese on top of that. Make another layer and add 1 can of water.

Cook over low heat until beans are tender.

Serves 6.

STUFFED ROUND STEAK

Mrs. Sam Bello

"The Italian name for this dish is "braciola." I would call them 'rolls of heaven.' My cousin (Joseph "Joe" Magliocca) made this dish with perfection. So delicious on top of your favorite macaroni. Yum, yum, yum!"
– MaryAnn Rotolo

2 round steaks (3 lb.)
Salt and pepper
Paprika
1/2 lb. sliced mushrooms (canned)
Pimento olives
Bread crumbs
1/2 c. melted oleo or bacon drippings
1 Tbsp. boiling water

Rolls:
Rub in salt, pepper and plenty of paprika. Overlap steaks, making one large one. Sprinkle steaks with 1/2 pound sliced mushrooms. Blanket with a layer of thinly sliced onion. Add pimentos (optional). Cover with fine bread crumbs. Beat 1/2 cup melted oleo or bacon drippings, 1 tablespoon boiling water and 1 egg. Immediately dribble mixture over bread crumbs. Arrange stuffed olives in a row on long side of steak. Bring the roll of meat around olives. Tie roll firmly. Roll in flour. Brown in 1/4 cup oleo or bacon. Sprinkle with salt, pepper and paprika. Add 1 cup red wine. Roast at 350° for 2 hours. Serve hot or cold, sliced.

Serves 6.

CASSEROLE

BAKED CAULIFLOWER

Virginia C. Capponi

1 large head cauliflower or
3 (10 oz.) frozen pkg.
1/2 tsp. salt
1 (10 1/2 oz.) can condensed
cream of chicken soup
1 (4 oz.) pkg. shredded
Cheddar cheese
⅓ c. mayonnaise
¼ c. bread crumbs
1 tsp. curry powder (optional)

Preheat oven to 350°. Break cauliflower into florets. In covered saucepan over medium heat in 1 inch boiling water, cook cauliflower with salt for 10 minutes. Drain well.

In 2 quart casserole, stir soup, mayonnaise, cheese and curry powder.

Add cauliflower and mix well. Toss bread crumbs in melted butter and sprinkle on top.
Bake 30 minutes.

Makes 8 servings.

BAKED EGGPLANT

Mrs. Martina Ciccarelli

1 eggplant (about 1 pound)
4 hard boiled eggs, sliced
4 eggs, beaten
tomato sauce
½ lb. of provolone, cut into small pieces
grated Italian cheese
flour

Tomato sauce:
1 6 oz. can of tomato paste
1 chopped onion peel

Slice eggplant into circles. Add salt and pepper to beaten eggs in a bowl. Place flour in another bowl. Dip sliced eggplant in egg mixture and then cover in flour.

Place oil in a pan and begin to heat. Place sliced eggplant in hot oil until brown and crisp. Drain on paper towel and set aside.

Make tomato sauce. Brown onion in a little oil, then add paste, salt, pepper and about three cans of water. Let simmer for about half an hour.

Using a 9 inch Pyrex cake dish, place a little sauce and grated cheese on the bottom, then add a layer of fried eggplant. Top with sauce, grated cheese, hard boiled eggs, and provolone cheese. Repeat until you have your final layer. Then top with sauce and grated cheese.

Bake at 350° for 1 hour.

BAKED STUFFED EGGPLANT

Shelly Genovese

1 lg. eggplant
5 slices Italian bread
1 clove garlic, minced
1 c. grated cheese
1 c. tomato sauce
½ c. grated mozzarella cheese
Salt and pepper

Soak Italian bread in water and squeeze out excess water. Cut eggplant in half. Scrap out inside. Parboil the outside of eggplant for 5 minutes. Cube the inside and fry with oil. Mix cubes with all other ingredients. Fill eggplant shells with mixture. Pour half the sauce on bottom of baking dish and cover eggplant with second half. Top with mozzarella. Bake, covered, for ½ hour and uncover for the last 5 minutes at 350°.

BAKED STUFFED EGGPLANT

Mrs. Rose Lombino

2 eggplants
2 c. bread crumbs
¼ c. Italian cheese
1 garlic clove
¼ c. oil
1 egg
½ lb. hamburger
Salt and pepper to taste

Scoop out the centers of the eggplant and cut them up. Boil together with eggplant shells until tender.

Filling:
Fry garlic and hamburger in oil. Add salt and pepper and cut up eggplant centers. Then add breadcrumbs, cheese, and 1 whole egg. Mix together.

Fill eggplant shells with mixture and bake at 350° for 1 hour.

BEAN AND MUSHROOM CASSEROLE

Laurie Capponi

1 can cream of mushroom soup
1 can mushrooms, drained
1 can Durkee's onion rings
2 cans French green beans

Drain beans well and place in medium size baking dish. Add undiluted soup and mix well. Add ½ can onion rings and mix. Cover top with remaining onion rings. Bake at 350° for ½ hour.

BROCCOLI CASSEROLE

Virginia Capponi

3 pkg. frozen broccoli
½ c. butter
2 c. milk
⅔ c. water
4 oz. Pepperidge Farm dressing
3 Tbsp. flour
1 Tbsp. chicken bouillon pellets - level
6 Tbsp. butter, melted
⅔ c. chopped walnuts

Cook broccoli without salt. Place in a buttered casserole dish.

Make white sauce with milk, butter, pellets, and flour. Pour over broccoli.

Melt the butter and add to water.

Then add water and butter to dressing and nuts. Sprinkle mix on casserole.

Bake at 350° for 20 to 30 minutes.

Serves 12.

BROCCOLI CASSEROLE

Dolores Parry

2 pkg. chopped broccoli
1 c. Minute rice, cooked
1 (8 oz.) jar Cheez-Whiz
1 can cream of mushroom soup
1 medium onion
1 Tbsp. margarine

Cook broccoli in small amount of water. Sauté onion until soft and golden. Add all other ingredients and pour into buttered casserole dish. Sprinkle with paprika or bread crumbs.

Bake at 350° for 30 minutes.

EGGPLANTS, STUFFED AND ROLLED

Sue Ferlo

2 hard boiled eggs
2 c. tomato sauce
2 slightly beaten eggs
1 medium eggplant
2 c. bread crumbs
½ lb. Prosciutto
½ c. grated Parmesan cheese
½ lb. Mozzarella cheese
2 c. Crisco

Skin the eggplant, slice lengthwise in ⅛ inch slices. Dip slices in egg batter and then in bread crumbs and fry in Crisco. Let fried slices cool in refrigerator for couple of hours. Lay a slice of Prosciutto on each slice of eggplant. Chop hard boiled eggs and mix with grated cheese; add this to the top of the Prosciutto (Italian ham). Lay thin slices of Mozzarella cheese on top of chopped eggs and grated cheese. Roll each slice and fasten with toothpicks. Place in a baking dish. Pour sauce and remainder of grated cheese over the rolls of eggplant.

Bake in 350° oven for 10 minutes or until mozzarella cheese is melted.

EGGPLANT PARMESAN

Mrs. Agnes Fontana

1 medium eggplant
4 eggs
1 c. flour
½ c. oil
3 c. tomato sauce
Mozzarella cheese, sliced thin
Grated Parmesan cheese

Slice eggplant thinly and place in a large bowl. Sprinkle salt between layers and place a plate directly over eggplant. Let stand for about 4 hours, rinse and dry.

Dip each slice of eggplant into beaten egg, and then in flour. Fry the coated eggplant in oil (the oil will have to be replaced from time to time as it will dry up). After all the eggplant is fried place a layer of eggplant in a deep baking dish. Over this, place slices of mozzarella cheese, grated cheese, and sauce. Repeat the layer three times until all eggplant is used.

Bake at 350° for about 30 minutes.

EGG CASSEROLE

A. Guaspari

6 slices firm white bread, crumbled
½ lb. sharp cheddar cheese, crumbled
4 eggs, beaten
2 ½ c. milk
1 tsp. salt
1 tsp. dry mustard

Combine bread and cheese. Beat eggs and add milk, salt, and mustard. Pour over bread and cheese. Bake in buttered 1 ½ quart casserole at 325° for 1 ¼ hours.

Tastes best when made in advance and placed in the oven 1 ¼ hours before serving. (Could be mixed night before.) Great for company breakfast.

Serves 6.

E-Z POTATO CASSEROLE

Antoinette Guaspari

4 c. mashed potatoes
1 (8 oz.) pkg. softened cream cheese
Salt and pepper to taste
1 egg
1 onion

Beat the egg, mashed potatoes, and cream cheese. Add onions and seasoning. Place in a casserole dish. Bake at 350° for 45 minutes.

Can be prepared day before and baked next day.

FRESH VEGETABLE CASSEROLE

Kay Wilkinson

1 bunch broccoli, sliced lengthwise
2 c. mushrooms, sliced
1 large onion, chopped
1 can cream of mushroom soup
Salt & Pepper
Fresh dill or parsley

Layer vegetables, starting with broccoli. Season with salt, pepper and fresh dill or parsley. Pour the cream of mushroom soup over vegetables.

Bake at 400° for 30 minutes or until tender.

ITALIAN - SAUSAGE POLENTA PIE (Cornmeal and Sausage Pie)

Amy Breton

"I remember my Grandma Malorzo making polenta and serving it on her big macaroni (not 'pasta') board. Each of us had our own section, with sauce and lots of grated cheese – and, if available, meatballs and sausage." – Dolores (Malorzo) Ferlo

1 ½ lb. Italian sausage
1 c. sliced onion
1 clove garlic, crushed
1 (16oz.) can of tomatoes, undrained
1 (8 oz.) can of tomato sauce
¾ tsp. salt
½ tsp. oregano
½ tsp. sugar

¼ tsp. basil
⅛ tsp. pepper
¾ tsp. salt
1 ½ c. yellow cornmeal
1 c. grated sharp Cheddar cheese

Brown sausage in a large skillet. Reduce heat. Turning occasionally, cook sausage 15 minutes longer. Place on paper towels to drain. Pour off all but 1 tablespoon fat from the skillet and throw away excess.

In the remaining fat, sauté onions and garlic until golden brown, about 5 minutes. Cut 6 pieces of sausage in halves lengthwise and set aside for the top of the pie. Slice the remaining sausage into thin slices. Add tomatoes, tomato sauce, salt, oregano, sugar, basil, pepper, and sausage slices to the onion mixture in the skillet. Bring to a boil; reduce heat; simmer uncovered for 25 minutes and stirring occasionally.

Preheat oven to 375°. In a medium saucepan combine cornmeal with 3 cups water and ¾ teaspoon salt. Bring to a boil, stirring constantly, and boil until thickened, about 2 minutes. Remove from heat and let cool for about 5 minutes. Layer half the cornmeal mixture in a 2 ½ quart casserole. Top with half the sausage mixture. Sprinkle with half the cheese. Repeat layers. Arrange reserved sausage halves on top. Bake uncovered for 30 minutes or until heated through.

Makes 6 servings.

MEXICAN HOT STUFF

Margo Taylor

"My Mom and Dad were from South Dakota and Wisconsin of Irish/Scotch and German/English descendants who relocated to San Diego, CA, in the late 1950's. They never experienced ethnic foods such as Mexican, Asian, or even Italian growing up. Everything was "meat and potatoes." Mom was adventurous and liked trying new things, and this recipe of hers is one of our favorites. She called it 'Mexican Hot Stuff,' even though it's not really hot—just flavorful."

1 lb Lean Ground Beef
6-8 Corn Tortillas
16 oz. Sour Cream
1 Onion, chopped
1-2 Diced Green Chiles, canned, large
1-2 Diced Black Olives, canned
16 oz. Monterey Jack Cheese, shredded

Brown the ground beef and season with salt, pepper and garlic. To assemble the dish, take a corn tortilla, smear sour cream over it liberally. Place it in the bottom of a greased casserole dish. Next layer on the rest of the ingredients in the following order: cooked ground beef, chopped onion, diced green chiles, diced black olives, and Monterey Jack cheese. Repeat the entire process, pressing the layers down if you need to. End with the cheese on top. Cover with aluminum foil and bake at 350° F for 30-45 minutes until everything is hot and the cheese is melted. Stick under the broiler to get a nice brown look if you desire. Serve with additional salsa on the side. For a vegetarian version, use refried beans instead of the ground beef. Change the order of assembly as follows: corn tortilla, refried beans, sour cream, chopped onion, diced green onion, diced green chilies, diced black olives, and Monterey Jack cheese.

POLENTA

Mary Seccurra

1 cup cornmeal
1 cup cold water
1 pound pork, cut into cubes
2 cloves garlic
1 can tomato puree
Salt and pepper
Basil

Make the pork sauce first. Brown pork in olive oil; add garlic, tomato puree, salt, pepper, and basil and simmer for 2 hours.

When sauce is ready mix the cornmeal with cold water and stir well. Then, boil 3 cups of water and add cornmeal and stir. Cook until thick.

Serve polenta in a dish and pour bits of pork sauce on it.

SPINACH CASSEROLE

Dolores Parry

3 pkg. chopped spinach
1 ½ c. sour cream
1 pkg. dry onion soup
½ c. bread crumbs (plain)
¼ c. grated cheese
2 Tbsp. butter

Boil spinach and drain in a sieve. Mix onion soup and sour cream together. Mix bread crumbs, cheese and butter and sprinkle on top.

Bake at 325° uncovered for 30 minutes.

SPANISH RICE

Delcie Castro

1 lb. cut up chicken*
1 lb. sausage, or
1 lb. shrimp
1 or 2 green peppers
1 onion
1 can mushrooms

2 or 3 chicken bouillon cubes**
Pinch of saffron**
2 c. rice (Uncle Ben's)
2 c. water
1 c. tomatoes
Salt, pepper, garlic powder to taste

*Use as many pieces of chicken and sausage as size of family is needed.
**Do not use these ingredients with shrimp dish.

Brown garlic in a little oil and add chicken, sausage (or shrimp) until brown.
Remove from skillet and in same oil add peppers, onion and mushrooms until
softened a little. Add the 1 cup whole tomatoes and cook for 2 minutes over low heat.
Add rice, season to taste and cook 5 minutes longer.

In separate pot, boil 2 cups water and bouillon cubes. Then to rice mixture add water and meats and cook for
5 minutes. Cook in preheated oven 300° for 30 to 40 minutes in covered skillet. If rice is too dry, add more
tomatoes or water. Ten minutes before done, add peas.

Bake at 400° for 30 minutes or until tender.

STUFFED PEPPERS

Mrs. Martina Ciciarelli

8 green peppers
2 lb. ground pork
1 slice of stale Italian bread
4 eggs
1 c. grated Italian cheese
tomato, sauce

Tomato Sauce:
2 6 oz. cans tomato paste
1 chopped onion
salt and pepper

Wash peppers, cut them in
halves and remove seeds.
Sprinkle peppers with salt.

Mix pork, eggs, salt, pepper,
grated cheese, and the inside
of the stale bread moistened
with a little water. Fill each half
pepper with mixture.
Next make your sauce. Brown
onion in little olive oil, then
add tomato paste, salt, and
pepper, and about two cups of
water. Cook for half an hour.

Allow sauce to cool.

Place cooled sauce over
stuffed peppers.

In a large roaster, place
peppers with filling side up
and cover with sauce. If
necessary, add water to cover
the bottom of the peppers.
Bake at 450° for 1 hour.

STUFFED PEPPERS WITH BREAD STUFFING AND ANCHOVIES

Marie George

12 cubanelle peppers (light green peppers), cored and seeds removed. Set aside.

In large bowl:
1½ loaves bread cubes
3 cloves garlic, chopped fine
½ c. grated Romano cheese
½ tsp. dry parsley

1 can anchovies, chopped
½ bottle chopped
Spanish olives
½ c. cooking oil (set aside)
½ tsp. dry basil

Sprinkle water (½-1 cup) over bread cubes and ingredients until moist. Pour oil over ingredients, little at a time, til well blended; toss. Fill peppers with stuffing. Place in baking dish. Pour oil over peppers (¼-½ cup).

Cover with foil; bake 15 minutes or till peppers brown a little on top.

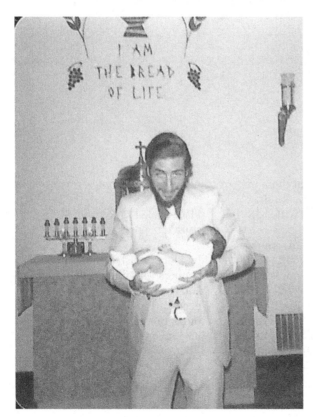

Anthony Gotti holding Donald, 1979

Christmas Program 1965

CHICKEN

• •

"I remember when Mr. Hinman would come around the East Rome neighborhood selling live chickens. You would pick the one you wanted from the back of the crate, then proceed to walk home carrying the chicken you chose, by its feet. We'd go in the back yard to cut off its head, fill a large pot of water on the stove and bring to a boil. The chicken was then placed in the pot for a few minutes. When done, it was time to clean the chicken. Pull the feathers out, clean in/out, and wow if you got an egg! Chicken was then cut up and was ready to cook."
-Lucille Hilts

APRICOT CHICKEN
....
Virginia Pisano

1 (12 oz.) jar apricot preserves
1 (8 oz.) bottle French dressing
1 envelope onion soup

Mix above and pour over chicken.

Bake uncovered at 350° about 2 hours or until nicely browned. Use above amounts according to the amount of chicken.

This makes enough for 2 fryers or parts.

BAKED CHICKEN AND SAUSAGE
....
Luguinia Curcio

2 lb. chicken
½ tsp. garlic salt
1 lb. sausage
1 ½ tsp. salt
6 medium potatoes
½ tsp. pepper
1 tsp. each oregano and paprika
⅓ c. vegetable oil

Arrange potatoes (quartered) in a shallow pan. Sprinkle ⅓ of seasoning mixture on the potatoes. Arrange chicken and sausage on top. Pour oil over all ingredients. Sprinkle on remaining seasonings.

Cover and bake in 420° oven for 1 hour. Turn oven down to 375° for an additional 30 minutes.

BATTER DIPPED CHICKEN
....
Mrs. Josephine Bird

1 (2 1/2 lb.) frying chicken
2 tsp. sugar
1 egg
2 tsp. salt
⅔ c. water
¾ c. flour
¼ c. Crisco oil
1 ½ c. Crisco oil

Beat together egg, water and ¼ cup Crisco oil. Add sugar, salt and flour. Mix until smooth.

Dip chicken, one piece at a time, into batter and fry about 23 minutes in an uncovered skillet with 1 ½ cups Crisco oil heated to 350°. Turn chicken often for even browning.

For spicier chicken, add 1 teaspoon paprika and ¼ teaspoon pepper to batter.

BISHOP MUGAUERO'S CHICKEN

Virginia Capponi

Whole chicken
Breadcrumbs
Olive oil
Salt and pepper
Parmesan cheese
2 or 3 bay leaves
Dry white wine

Cut up 1 whole chicken. Dip chicken parts in olive oil and then in bread crumbs mixed with salt, pepper, and Parmesan cheese.

Place chicken in one shallow layer in a baking dish. Add leaves on top of chicken. Add dry white wine to the dish, but not on the chicken - rather pour into the dish.

Bake at 350° for about 1 hour.

As the pieces brown, add more wine. Serve with pan juices.

CHICKEN BREASTS

Ange Amoroso

8 boned chicken breasts
Bread crumbs, mixed with cheese, parsley, salt, pepper, garlic powder
2 eggs, beaten
Flour
4 cans mushrooms, drained
1 c. sherry or white wine
1 c. mushroom liquid

Dip breasts in flour, beaten egg, then bread crumbs - fry. Put cutlets in a shallow pan. Pour mixture of wine and mushroom liquid and garlic powder over breasts. Spread mushrooms over all. Cover. Bake at 325° for 45 or 50 minutes.

CHICKEN CACCIATORE

Mrs. Josephine Bird

2 lbs. chicken parts
2 Tbsp. shortening
1 (10 3/4 oz.) can tomato sauce
¼ c. dry red wine
½ c. onion, chopped
2 large garlic cloves, minced
1 tsp. crushed oregano
¼ tsp. salt
½ green pepper, cut in strips

In a skillet, brown chicken in shortening; pour off fat. Add remaining ingredients, except pepper. Cover, cook over low heat for 30 minutes. Add pepper; cook 15 minutes more. Stir now and then.

CITY CHICKEN ON SKEWERS

Marie George

2 lb. veal, cubed
2 lb. pork, cubed
Salt, pepper, parsley, and garlic salt

Marinate overnight in refrigerator.
Next day: 40 skewers (size 5-6 inches long).
1. Prepare dish with 3 eggs, beaten, grated cheese, salt, pepper and parsley.
2. Prepare another dish with 2 cups flour, salt and pepper.
3. Alternate on skewer, 1 piece veal and 1 piece pork (4 pieces on each skewer).
4. Roll in egg batter, roll in flour and fry. After all is fried, bake for ½ hour at 350°.

Makes 40.

CHICKEN IN OVEN (Or Baked Chicken)

A. Guaspari

6 medium potatoes, peeled and quartered
1 tsp. each oregano and paprika
½ tsp. garlic salt
½ tsp. pepper
1 ½ tsp. salt
1 frying chicken, cut up
1 lb. Italian sausage, cut up
⅓ c. oil

Arrange potatoes in shallow casserole dish (3 quart size). Mix seasoning and sprinkle half on potatoes. Arrange chicken and sausage on top. Pour oil over mixture and sprinkle with remainder of seasonings.

Cover and bake in 425° oven for 1 hour. Reduce heat to 375° and uncover and bake for 30 minutes longer or until chicken and potatoes are well-browned.

CHICKEN LIVERS

Bev Zigrino

1 lb. chicken liver
1 egg, beaten
Crackers or bread crumbs
Salt and pepper

1. Use frying pan with enough oil to cover bottom of pan.
2. Dip liver in beaten egg.
3. Roll in crumbs.
4. Place in pan, fry until coating is brown and liver is tender, about 35 minutes, over medium heat.

CHICKEN LIVERS ON TOAST (Crostini alia Fiorentina)

Amy Breton

½ lb. chicken livers
2 to 3 fresh sage leaves
2 Tbsp. oil
Black pepper (pinch)
2 Tbsp. finely chopped onion
4 slices lightly toasted bread

Wash the livers, removing any tissue, and pat dry. Chop very fine.

Heat oil and sauté onion and sage leaves until onion is soft and beginning to brown.

Remove sage. Place chopped livers into a skillet, season with pepper; cook over low heat until livers are cooked and no pink color remains.

Spread mixture on the toast and serve at once.

GRANDMA'S CHICKEN OREGANATO

Barbara Amoroso

"I never had the pleasure of meeting my husband's grandma, Lucy "Lizzie" Amoroso, but I know she made this recipe with a lot of love. When I make her recipe, I feel she is with me in the kitchen. Everyone that has tasted this recipe loves it!"

Cut up chicken in pieces. I use bone-in breasts with the skin removed and cut in half. Salt and pepper each piece and fry in olive oil in a heavy, deep saucepan on medium high heat (a few pieces at a time, so they don't touch) until brown. After all the pieces are fried, put all of them back in the pan. Add ½ cup of water and then add lots of fresh cut up basil and Italian parsley, about 2 Tbsp. oregano, 2 bay leaves and lots of cracked black pepper. Put the cover on and turn the chicken from time to time. Cook for about ½ hour and enjoy!

STEAMED CHICKEN WITH ONIONS

Mrs. Angeline Messineo

3 ½ to 4 lb. fowl
salt and pepper
½ c. flour
1 to 2 c. liquids
4 Tbsp salad oil or shortening
1 c. sliced onions

Cut fowl into pieces for serving. Wash under running water or wipe with a wet cloth and dry thoroughly. Sprinkle with salt and pepper and dredge in flour.

Heat fat in a heavy skillet. Brown the chicken in the hot oil. Next, brown onions in the same pan. When the chicken is almost browned remove any excess grease, and then add liquid according to taste.

Cover tightly and simmer over low heat for 1 hour or until chicken is tender.

Parsley may be added desired.

CREAMED CHICKEN WITH BISCUITS

Mrs. Mary Ringlund

Melt 6 Tbsp. butter or chicken fat. Blend in:

6 Tbsp. flour
1 tsp. salt
⅛ tsp. pepper

Cook over low heat until bubbling. Remove from heat and stir in:

1 ½ c. well-seasoned chicken broth
1 c. cream or top of milk

Bring to a boil and boil for one minute stirring it constantly.

Gently stir in:

1 c. cut-up, cooked chicken.

Just before serving, add 2 Tbsp. sherry flavoring, if desired.

Serve over hot biscuits below:

2 c. sifted flour
1 tsp. Salt
3 tsp. Double action baking powder
⅓ c. oil
⅔ c. milk

Preheat over to 450°. Add flour, salt, and baking powder into a bowl, but do not stir together. Add in oil and milk and stir with a fork until mixed, or until you can clean the sides of the bowl and the dough rounds up into a ball.

Drop Tbsps. of dough onto an ungreased cookie sheet and bake for 10 to 12 minutes.

Makes about 16 biscuits.

FATHER CLEMENTE'S CHICKEN

Fr. Joseph Clemente

4 skinless, boneless chicken breast halves
1 (10-oz.) bottle Worcestershire sauce
2 T. butter
8 slices cooked bacon
1 (8-oz.) pkg. Monterey Jack cheese, shredded
1 (16-oz.) ctn. honey mustard salad dressing
8 oz. fresh mushrooms, sliced

To marinate: Place chicken in a glass dish or bowl; poke chicken with a fork several times, then pour Worcestershire sauce in and turn to coat.

Cover dish or bowl and refrigerate for about 1 hour. Preheat oven to broil.

Heat butter in small skillet over medium heat. Add onions and sauté for about 10 minutes or until soft; set aside.

Remove chicken from marinade (discard any remaining liquid) and broil for about 5 minutes on each side. When chicken is almost finished, top each breast with 2 slices bacon, then cheese. Continue to broil until cheese has melted, then remove from oven.

Serve with mushrooms in a bowl and salad dressing for topping.

FRIED CHICKEN

Nancy Paciencia

4 chicken breasts
1 c. flour
French's seasoning salt
1 tsp. garlic salt
1 tsp. parsley
Oil
Wishbone Italian salad dressing

Clean chicken and marinate in salad dressing for at least 4 hours. Half an hour before serving, combine flour with enough seasoning salt to make the flour slightly orange, garlic salt, and parsley. Put on waxed paper.

Roll chicken in flour mixture until coated. Heat oil in frying pan - oil should be ¼ inch deep. Place coated chicken in heated oil and fry until golden brown (each side should take 10 minutes on medium heat).

For even tastier chicken, put some of the Italian dressing in the oil.

UNCLE RONNIE'S CHICKEN

Margo Taylor

"My Uncle Ronnie was quite the cook in his day, working at various bars, restaurants and taverns. One of the many recipes he shared with me is the chicken dish below. I've lovingly named it after him."

2 lbs Chicken Breasts/Tenders, boneless, skinless
1 Wishbone Russian Dressing
1 Lipton Onion Soup envelope
1 20 oz. can pineapple chunks

Place chicken in slow cooker. In a small bowl, mix together entire bottle of Russian Dressing, 1 envelope of Lipton Onion Soup, and juice from pineapple can. Add drained pineapple to slow cooker.

Pour sauce over the chicken breasts and pineapple.

Cook on low heat for 6-8 hours or high 4 hours.

Serve with rice.

ST. JOHN'S CONFRATERNITY
Fourth Annual Dance
Y. M. C. A. GYM, ROME
Monday Eve., June 4th, 1945
Louis Armstrong and His Orchestra
Radio and Recording Artists
Dancing 8 to 12
ckets $3.12   Tax .63   Total $3.75

FISH

BAKED FISH

Gloria Panara

2 Ibs. fresh fillet of haddock
Parsley
Olive oil
Parmesan cheese
4-5 slices (3 or 4 day-old) white bread (in blender)
1-2 T. fresh lemon juice
Salt and pepper

Wash and check fish in cold water (don't pat dry). Place in a greased baking dish. Sprinkle lemon juice over all.

In a bowl, place bread crumbs, salt, pepper, parsley and 2-3 tablespoons Parmesan cheese; mix well. Sprinkle over fish evenly; drizzle olive oil over this and bake at 350° for 20 minutes to ½ hour.

Drop Tbsps. of dough onto an ungreased cookie sheet and bake for 10 to 12 minutes.

Makes about 16 biscuits.

BAKED FISH ITALIAN

Anna Brasachio

4 Tbsp. margarine
½ lb. sliced mushrooms, or
1 c. canned mushrooms
2 Tbsp. sliced green onions
4 freshwater trout
2 Tbsp. minced parsley
Salt and pepper to taste
4 Tbsp. fine dry bread crumbs

Grease a shallow baking dish with margarine and place the fish. Add sliced mushrooms, onion and 1 tablespoon of parsley. Season with salt and pepper. Dot with some of the margarine.

Melt the rest of the margarine and mix with the bread crumbs.

Place this over the mushrooms.

Bake in moderately hot (375°) oven for 20 to 25 minutes, or until the fish is tender and crumbs are light brown.

Sprinkle with rest of parsley and garnish with lemon quarters.

Makes 4 servings.

BAKED HALIBUT STEAK

Mrs. Philomena Vito

"My father loved all kinds of fish. In fact, he was quite a fisherman in his youth. I'm sure he enjoyed halibut because it's a lean, mild, and sweet tasting white fish. It's very good on its own, but the secret to this baked fish is the anchovy sauce." - MaryAnn Rotolo

2 lbs. halibut steak
¼ c. butter or margarine
1 tsp. salt
¼ tsp. sweet basil
2 Tbsp. lemon juice

Preheat oven to 350°. If steaks are frozen, thaw, and patch dry with a paper towel.

Melt butter or margarine, add lemon juice and basil to butter. Place steaks in a greased, shallow baking dish. Sprinkle steaks with salt and brush generously with fat mixture. Bake for 30 minutes or until steak is easily flaked with fork.

Baste several times with fat.

Serve with anchovy sauce:
8 anchovy fillets
2 Tbsp. salad or olive oil
2 Tbsp. flour
1 c. milk
2 Tbsp. lemon juice
½ tsp. salt
⅛ tsp. pepper

Chop anchovies in small pieces. Heat oil, and then stir in flour. Gradually stir in milk, and cook, stirring constantly until sauce thickens.

Add lemon juice, salt, pepper, add anchovy fillets. Pour sauce over fish steaks or serve separately topped with chopped parsley.

Makes about 1 c. sauce.

BAKED STUFFED FILLET

Sue Ferlo

2 lbs. fillets of your choice
2 c. bread crumbs
1/2 tsp. sage
1/2 tsp. thyme
1 tsp. salt
1/4 tsp. black pepper
4 Tbsp. water
1 can tomato sauce

Mix all ingredients together (except fish) in a bowl. Place fillets flat and pour equal amounts of stuffing mixture on each one. Roll fillets in jelly roll fashion and secure with a toothpick. Place on a greased shallow pan. Pour tomato sauce over the rolls. Bake at 375° for 20 to 25 minutes or until flaky when broken with a fork.

BEST FISH EVER

Fr. John Wood

2 lbs. fish (filet of sole, haddock or scrod)
dry parsley
Crackers, crumbled
1½ sticks margarine or butter
Salt and pepper
¾ c. sour cream
Garlic powder

Wash fish; pat dry. With whisk, mix melted butter with sour cream. Spread a portion of sour cream and butter mixture to cover the bottom of a long baking pan. Put fish on top. Put the remaining cream mixture on top of fish and spread evenly. Sprinkle salt and pepper, cracker crumbs, parsley and garlic evenly on top in that order.

Bake at 375° for 20 to 25 minutes or until fish easily breaks apart with fork.

Note: Melted butter and sour cream mixture should not be too thick, but easy to spread. If too thick, add more melted butter to mixture and whisk a bit. If too thin, add more sour cream.

Father John Wood with Altar Servers

CALAMARI RIPIENI STUFATE AL VINO BIANCO
(Stuffed Squid Braised In White Wine)

Lucille Argenzia

6 large squid

Clean squid by removing sac and skin from tentacles; rinse until water is very clean; dice tentacles very fine.

Stuffing:
1 T. olive oil
½ tsp. finely chopped garlic or more to taste
1 egg, well-beaten
Pepper to taste
2 T. diced parsley
2½ tsp. Parmesan cheese
½ tsp. salt
¼ c. fine bread crumbs

Mix stuffing ingredients together until smooth; add more olive oil if needed to make smooth and glossy. Add diced tentacles and blend well. Divide stuffing into 6 portions. Fill pockets. Do not overstuff as squid shrinks as it cooks; be sure to sew the ends closed.

Using a large nonstick skillet, lay squid in a single layer; first sauté lightly in olive oil and add a little garlic, then turn over. Brown squid on all sides. Cover tightly and cook for 30 to 40 minutes in braising liquid. Remove squid and store in refrigerator until ready to serve. Reserve all liquid.

To Reheat: Warm a nonstick skillet; add liquid and squid; leave in skillet only until warm enough to serve. Braising Liquid: Put enough olive oil in a 6 or 7-inch skillet to measure about ¼ inch. Add 1 cup coarsely chopped plum tomatoes and juice. Add 4 whole garlic cloves. Add 1 cup of dry white wine. Bring to a boil and simmer about 5 minutes. This can be done ahead of time.

DEEP FRIED FISH

Mrs. Evelyn Schmidt

1 c. flour
1 tsp. baking powder
1 tsp. salt
¾ c. milk
1 egg

Sprinkle fish with salt. Mix ingredients. Coat the fish and deep fry 3 minutes and then turn for 3 minutes more at 375°. Drain.

FISH STEAKS IN BEER

Sue Ferlo

1 ½ lb. boneless fish steaks
2 cans beer
1 onion, diced
1 lime
2 bay leaves
2 Tbsp. butter
½ tsp. paprika
2 Tbsp. flour
½ tsp. seasoned salt
½ tsp. pepper

Lay fish steaks in a heavy saucepan with cover. Pour beer over fish; add onion, diced, and lime, cut in half, bay leaves and seasoned salt. Bring to a boil, then turn heat low. Cover and simmer 5 minutes. Remove cover and simmer 5 minutes more.

Lift fish steaks out of broth. Discard onion, bay leaves and lime. Blend the butter and flour into a smooth paste. Add to broth, stirring constantly until thick. Add pepper and fish steaks to sauce and simmer just long enough to re-heat fish.

Serve with rice; 4 to 6 servings.

FISH STEW (Burrida)

Sue Ferlo

4 Tbsp. olive oil
1 onion, chopped
1 carrot, chopped
1 stalk celery, chopped
1 clove garlic, crushed
1 Tbsp. chopped parsley
1 to 2 anchovy fillets, chopped

1 sole, filet and cut into strips
1 lb. eel, cut in 2 inch slices
Salt and pepper
1 (8 oz.) can tomatoes
½ c. white wine
½ c. water
½ tsp. chopped basil

1 mackerel, cleaned and cut into thick slices
6 to 8 oz. halibut filet, cut into strips
4 oz. shrimp, frozen or fresh
4 slices Italian bread

Heat oil in large shallow skillet. Add onion, garlic, celery, carrot, parsley and anchovy. Cook for 5 minutes. Add tomatoes, wine, water, a little pepper and the basil. Cover and simmer for 15 minutes. Add the prepared mackerel, sole, halibut and eel. Cover and simmer gently for 20 to 30 minutes, adding more wine or water, if needed. Add the shrimp; cook another 5 minutes.

Grill or toast the bread slices and place them in large deep soup plates. Place the fish stew in the bowls and serve hot.

SHRIMP CREOLE

Jennie Jackson

"I remember my first time making this dish. My husband was on a seafood "kick" at the time, so I decided to try it out. My hubby was enjoying it over brown rice, but after a few mouthfuls his face went green—I'd missed removing a shell off of a shrimp! He hasn't eaten shrimp since! The moral of the story: be sure to double check your shrimp or use peeled frozen!" – MaryAnn Rotolo

Saute for three minutes:
1 lb. cooked and cleaned shrimp
or one package of frozen shrimp
4 Tbsp. shortening

Lift out shrimp, and add to remaining shortening:

1 stalk celery, diced
1 small onion, diced
1 green pepper, diced
½ lb. mushrooms, sliced
1 clove of garlic, if desired

Saute until highly browned. Add:
6 peeled tomatoes or 2 oz. can of tomatoes
Dash of pepper
Crumbled bay leaf
1 tsp. salt
Dash of cayenne

Simmer for 20 minutes or until thickened. Add shrimp, reheat and serve with fluffy cooked rice.

Variations: use cream of mushroom soup instead of tomatoes, and use whole bay leaf and remove after it suits to taste.

STEWED EELS (Anguille Umido)

Amy Breton

1 ½ lb. eel
1 onion, sliced
1 clove garlic, crushed
1 carrot, chopped
5 to 6 mushrooms, sliced
Olive oil
¼ pt. (½ c.) white wine
½ c. water
1 bay leaf
Chopped parsley
Salt and pepper

Cut skinned eels into 2 inch lengths. Heat some oil in a skillet. Saute onion, garlic and carrot until soft. Add mushrooms and cook for 2 to 3 minutes. Add the eel, wine and water. This should just cover the fish. Add the bay leaf and seasoning.

Cover and cook gently until the eel is tender, usually about 30 minutes.

Serve sprinkled with chopped parsley.

STUFFED SQUID (Calamari)

Agnes Fontana

8 small squid
1 tsp. chopped parsley
1 beaten egg
1 ½ c. bread crumbs
Salt, pepper, and garlic salt

Sauce:
1 (No. 2) can tomatoes
1 clove garlic

Clean squid thoroughly. Wash well and drain. Combine remaining ingredients and fill cavities in each squid. Sew squid.

Saute garlic in hot oil until browned. Remove garlic. Add tomatoes and cook down for about 1/2 hour. Add squid and continue cooking for another 45 minutes.

Serve whole.

"I remember our father (Alfred "Pops" Magnanti) would have to go to our basement kitchen stove to make tripe because of the stink! Once it was done, he added it to the fresh sauce that my mom (Rosie) made. With fresh Italian bread, it was enjoyed by the whole family. He was well into his 80s when it became too much work for him to make. He would help the guys down at the Toccolana Club make it and would bring some home to enjoy."
- Rosemary Magnanti and Peggy "Magnanti" Demers

"I remember having to clean all the fish on Christmas Eve. It was a job I did not enjoy. We bought the eel from Stan's Seafood and had him skin it for us. A tradition my son still carries on." -Mary Natalie

TRIPE IN TOMATO SAUCE

Angeline Gualteri

3 lb. tripe
1 (16 oz.) can tomato sauce or crushed tomatoes
1 tsp. rosemary
1 tsp. mint leaves
1 clove garlic
½ glass wine or wine vinegar
1 Tbsp. salt
Black pepper to taste

Boil tripe. Cut off fat and cut in strips. Fry oil and garlic. Add tripe and fry for 15 minutes. Drain tripe in a strainer to drain off the oil. Put tripe in a saucepan; add tomato sauce or crushed tomatoes; add small amount of water. Also add rosemary, mint leaves, salt and black pepper; 1/2 glass of wine or 1/2 glass wine vinegar. Cook until tender. Add more water if needed.

You can add cut potatoes, if desired.

"Our mother, Mary (Magnanti) McGowan would have "Tripe Parties." All her brothers and sisters would come over to enjoy it. Once our mom passed, and when we would come to Rome to visit, we would buy the tripe at an Italian store in Schenectady and take it over to Uncle Pops to make for us. We really appreciated him making it for us and we enjoyed being with him, Aunt Rosie and my cousin Peggy while eating it. The next generation continued making it with our brother Mark learning from my mother. Sadly, he has also passed." - Pat McGowan Baumeister and MaryBeth McGowan

TRIPE STEW

Barbara Biamonte

2 lb. honeycomb tripe
¼ c. oil
1 large onion, chopped
1 clove garlic, chopped
½ c. celery
2 to 3 green peppers, chopped
1 tsp. parsley
½ tsp. basil
1 bay leaf
1 (No. 2 1/2) can crushed tomatoes
½ c. burgundy wine
½ tsp. baking soda

Soak the tripe overnight in a salt and water or lemon juice and water mixture. Wash and bring to a boil with baking soda. Wash again and cut in cubes. Saute but don't brown. Add tomatoes, vegetable, seasonings, and wine and cook for 1 hour, or until tender.

TUNA CASSEROLE

Mrs. Henry Baptiste

1 bag medium egg noddles
1 can tuna, shredded
1 can cream of mushroom soup
Milk
Butter

Boil egg noodles.

In a baking dish add tuna and cream of mushroom soup and blend together. Stir in cooked noodles and cover with milk and dabs of butter.

Cook in an oven until baked.

Some like it moist and juicy, so, use your own judgment.

TUNA FRITTERS

Bev Zigrino

1 large can tuna
15 saltine crackers
1 egg

1. Use frying pan with enough oil to cover bottom of pan.
2. Put tuna in bowl.
3. Crumble crackers.
4. Add egg.
5. Mix all together.
6. Make into patties.
7. Place in frying pan; cook until golden brown on both sides, about 15 to 20 minutes.

Nº 32130

NAME

ADDRESS

CITY

Seller's Name

Address

HOLDER OF THIS TICKET HAS ONE SHARE IN THE DRAWING OF THE FOLLOWING TO BE GIVEN AWAY AT

ST. JOHN'S PARISH FESTIVAL

JULY 1, 1950—12½" TELEVISION SET
JULY 2, 1950—12½" TELEVISION SET
JULY 3, 1950—12½" TELEVISION SET
JULY 4, 1950—NEW 1950 BUICK

Seller of Ticket Winning Car will Receive a 16" Television Set

Winner need not be present at the Drawing on July 4

Nº 32130

TICKET 50¢

CHICKEN (OR SHRIMP) SCAMPI

Mary Fahey

1 lb. boneless chicken breast
1 egg, beaten
1 c. Italian bread crumbs
½ tsp. salt
¼ tsp. pepper
½ c. oil
1 lb. linguini
1 lemon, cut up

Sauce:
1 c. butter
½ tsp. parsley
6 cloves garlic, minced
1 tsp. salt
1 T. lemon juice
1 tsp. pepper

Cut chicken into cubes, dip in egg, and bread crumbs. Fry until brown.

Cook pasta.

Make sauce and toss chicken in sauce. Add chicken and sauce to macaroni. Toss again.

Serve with lemon wedge.

MaryAnn Rotolo, Mary Natalie

MACARONI

• •

FETTUCCINE ALFREDO

Delcie Castro

1 c. fettuccine
1 Tbsp. oil
¼ lb. sweet butter
¾ c. grated Parmesan cheese
½ c. rich, fresh sweet cream
1 egg, lightly beaten
Salt and freshly ground black pepper

Cook noodles until tender, 8 to 10 minutes, in salted boiling water with 1 tablespoon oil added to prevent sticking. Drain thoroughly in colander.

Melt butter in chafing dish, or in kettle over medium heat. Add cheese, cream, beaten egg gradually and blend until slightly thickened. Add noodles, salt and freshly ground black pepper to taste and toss lightly until noodles are coated evenly with sauce.

Serve on hot plates and garnish with additional cheese.

FETTUCCINI MUSHROOM CARBONARA

Angie Money

¼ lb. bacon
¼ c. milk (room temp.)
½ lb. sliced fresh mushrooms
½ c. grated Parmesan cheese
8 oz. fettuccini, uncooked
2 eggs, slightly beaten
¼ c. butter or margarine, softened
2 tsp. chopped parsley
Salt and pepper to taste

Sauté bacon until crisp; drain, reserving drippings. Crumble bacon; set aside. Sauté mushrooms in reserved bacon drippings until tender; set aside. Meanwhile, cook fettuccini according to package directions. Drain well and place in warm serving dish large enough for tossing. Add crumbled bacon; sauté mushrooms and butter or margarine, milk, grated cheese, eggs and parsley. Toss until fettuccini is well coated.

Salt and pepper to taste.

Makes 4-6 servings.

GNOCCHI

Elizabeth Voci

"Whenever I saw my mother take out her macaroni board and put it on the table, I knew it was time to make the gnocchi. I would sit there and watch her as she put the ingredients on the table, put her hairnet on, and start the process. When she first started making gnocchi she used real potatoes. They would be peeled, boiled, then she would put them through a ricer (which I still have). Not sure when she changed to instant potatoes but the gnocchi came out much lighter and we didn't call them "sinkers" after that.

Mom would mix the ingredients together on the board until the dough was formed. We would take some dough and roll it out into a long snakelike piece on a lightly floured board, then cut it into about 1 inch pieces. Then the fun began. We would take our thumb and put it in the middle of the 1 inch piece and "flick and roll" it into the gnocchi. You can also use a fork or gnocchi board to make ridges if you want. If you are not eating This recipe makes enough that she would supply her family and neighbors with some. To this day, people still tell me that my mom's gnocchi were the best."

5 c. Instant Potatoes
4 c. Hot tap water
1 beaten egg
6 c. flour

Mix potatoes and water. Let cool.

Add egg and flour. Move dough to a lightly floured board and break into pieces. You can also use a fork or gnocchi board to make ridges if you want. If you are not eating them right away, put them on a baking sheet with parchment paper and set in the freezer for 15 minutes, then put in the freezer bag. When ready to eat them, boil water, place gnocchi in a pot. When they rise to the top they should be cooked, about 5-6 minutes.

LINGUINE WITH BACCALA IN RED SAUCE

MaryAnn Rotolo

1 lb. Linguine
1 lb. Baccalà (Dried and Salted Cod)
1 sm. Onion, chopped

¼ Olive Oil
28 oz. canned crushed tomatoes
½ tsp. red pepper flakes, to taste
¼ cup capers

1 small handful chopped fresh parsley (optional)

Soak baccala in cold water, (typically for 3 days with occasional water changes). Meanwhile in a medium pot over medium high heat, fry the onion in olive oil until softened, about 3- 5 minutes. Add the crushed tomatoes and red pepper flakes. Continue to cook sauce. When sauce comes to slow bubbling (bubbles pop through) add pieces of the baccala, cut into size portions of your liking. Cover loosely and simmer gently for 20-30 minutes. Check seasoning, adding salt and more crushed pepper as desired. Finish with capers and parsley. Cook pasta per instructions. Serve baccala sauce and over pasta.

MACARONI AND CHEESE

Mary F. Lanzi

1 lb. elbow macaroni
2 Tbsp. butter
2 Tbsp. flour
1 tsp. salt
¼ c. buttered bread crumbs
¼ tsp. paprika
2 ½ c. hot milk
1 ½ c. shredded Cheddar cheese

Cook elbows as directed on package. Melt butter, blend in flour, salt; add hot milk; simmer 1 minute, stirring constantly. Add 1 cup shredded Cheddar cheese and stir until smooth. Combine elbows with sauce in baking dish.

Top with 1/2 cup shredded cheese, bread crumbs and paprika.

Bake uncovered in 375° oven for 25 minutes. Makes 6 servings.

MANICOTTI

Sue Ferlo

Batter:
4 eggs
1/4 tsp. salt
1 c. flour
1 c. water

Ricotta Filling:
2 lb. coarse Ricotta cheese
4 eggs
¾ tsp. salt
⅓ c. grated cheese
¼ tsp. black pepper
2 Tbsp, chopped parsley

Mix all together well.

Beat eggs slightly; add salt, water and blend together. Add flour and mix until smooth. Will be a thin batter. Heat pancake griddle on medium temperature and very lightly grease with thin coat of oil. It is not necessary to repeat this unless batter sticks to pan. Cook as you would pancakes.

Using a tablespoonful of batter, spread quickly to form a very thin circle. Will cook very fast. Turn once over lightly and remove immediately. Will make about 25 or 30 manicotti shells. Spread 1 tablespoon Ricotta filling in the center of shell and roll up. Place in shallow pan, making only 1 layer. Spread your favorite spaghetti sauce on top and sprinkle grated Mozzarella cheese over. Cover and bake at 375° for 20 to 25 minutes. Serve immediately.

You may use electric fry pan to fry manicotti shells at 375°.

NOODLES WITH CREAM (Tagliatelle alia Panna)

Amy Breton

1 lb. ribbon noodles
4 tsp. butter
2 egg yolks
1 c. grated Parmesan cheese
6 Tbsp. heavy cream
Black pepper to taste
Extra butter and grated cheese

This recipe is favored by those people that cannot eat the rich Italian tomato sauce.

Cook noodles in salted, boiling water until tender, but firm (al dente). Drain thoroughly and place into a large hot serving bowl. Add egg yolks, butter, and cream and toss in the noodles lightly until the heat from these ingredients has "cooked" the eggs and cream.

Add pepper and serve with extra butter and Parmesan cheese.

OIL AND GARLIC SAUCE WITH TUNA (Olio e Aglio con Tonno)

Carol Ceci

1 c. oil
8 cloves garlic, sliced thin
1 c. water
1 ½ Tbsp. parsley (dried fresh, chopped fine)
½ tsp. oregano
½ tsp. black pepper or
1 can tuna, drained

In a 10 inch skillet, heat oil and garlic until slightly brown. Stir water in slowly; simmer a few minutes. Add parsley, oregano, and black pepper. Simmer about 10 to 15 minutes. Remove from stove.

Add tuna, chopped fine and mix with 1 pound cooked spaghetti, 2 tablespoons grated Parmesan cheese.

Extra cheese and black pepper may be served for those who prefer extra seasoning.

"One of my favorite cooking memories is when my grandmother would get out the 3' x 3' wooden board. When I saw that I knew it was going to be a fun day! First we would have to make sure our hands were clean, then I would watch as a whole bag of flour was emptied onto the board. Then working her hands like magic, she would circle them round and round, pushing the flour into a volcanic looking crater. Then I would be allowed to crack eggs into the center. The farmer would save the green colored eggs just for me, so those were never used for baking. She would hover over me making sure no shells were accidently included. As she added other ingredients into the crater, I would watch eagerly waiting for an ingredient that she would let me pour in. When she was satisfied, it was time to begin. I would watch as she would smash the eggs and mix whatever she had entered into that center circle, waiting, just waiting until the messy wet globs were perfect. Then she would let me knead the little piece of dough that she would save just for me. Every time I make bread or pasta, the smells and the feeling of the dough, all those baking days together, remind me of my grandmother who always was willing to teach and let me help." – Carlene Corigliano

PASTA
....
Amalia Fusco

2 c. flour
2 eggs
2 Tbsp. oil
½ tsp. Salt

Place flour in a bowl, make a well and add egg, salt and oil. Mix well. Turn out onto a board and form into a ball. If it is too stiff, add cold water. (Sometimes 1 to 2 tablespoons will be needed to make pliable dough, but do not make it too soft.)

Knead the dough for 20 minutes or more, until smooth and elastic. Divide into half and roll out each section very thinly. Roll the flat sheet like a jelly roll and cut into 1/4 inch slices. Unfurl the slices and lay flat on a board sprinkled with flour. Allow to dry about 2 hours.

To cook: Drop into 3 quarts boiling salted water; boil for 5 to 10 minutes until tender. DO NOT OVERCOOK. (Always start with cold water and bring to a boil, as hot water from the pipes contain minerals from the pipes and change the taste of the pasta.)

Makes 1 lb. To make more, simply multiply the recipe as desired. This makes a sizable amount of dough and kneading may take longer.

MACARONI AND BEANS (Pasta e Fagioli)
....
Amy Breton

1 ½ c. dried beans (navy or pea)
1 lb. shell macaroni
1 clove garlic, crushed
2 c. diced and peeled tomatoes
1 tsp. sage
½ tsp. oregano
¼ tsp. pepper
Salt
3 Tbsp. olive oil
1 large onion, chopped
2 c. carrot, sliced
1 c. celery, chopped
Parsley, chopped
Grated Parmesan cheese

Combine beans with 6 cups cold water in a large bowl. Refrigerate overnight. Place beans and water in 6 quart kettle. Add 1 ½ teaspoons of salt. Bring to boil. Reduce heat, cover and simmer for about 3 hours (or until beans are tender). Stir several times during cooking. Drain but reserve the liquid which will be about 2 ½ cups. Cook macaroni separately as indicated on the package. In large skillet, saute onion, carrot, celery and garlic. Cover and cook until soft, about 20 minutes. Do not brown. Add tomato, sage, oregano, 1/2 teaspoon salt and the pepper. Cover and cook over medium heat for 15 minutes.

In large kettle combine beans, macaroni and sauteed vegetables. Add 1 ½ cups reserved bean liquid. Bring to boil; cover and simmer 35 to 40 minutes, stirring several times and adding more bean liquid, if necessary. Add salt and pepper to taste.

Place into serving dish. Sprinkle with chopped parsley and grated Parmesan cheese.

Makes 8 servings.

PASTA FAGIOLI OR PASTA CECI

Sue Ferlo

"I remember being served macaroni n' beans "pasta fagioli" twice a week in our home. My mother would occasionally switch up the dish by changing out the type of macaroni or beans. Ditialini to Small Shells, Garbanzo peas (ceci beans) or Cannellini white or red beans." – MaryAnn Rotolo

1 can red or white kidney beans or
1 can chickpeas
1 can 8 oz. Hunt's tomato sauce
½ can water
2 Tbsp, oil
1 garlic clove
Salt and pepper to taste
½ lb. Ditalini or small shells

Put oil in a 2-quart saucepot, add garlic, and brown. Remove garlic and add tomato sauce and 1/2 can of water. Simmer until oil rises to the top (30 to 45 minutes). Add beans. When the sauce is done, in a separate 3-quart saucepan, boil 2 quarts water. Add Ditalini and cook for 7 to 8 minutes. Drain macaroni and add to sauce with beans.

Simmer together for a few minutes and serve.

PASTA FAGIOLI

Angeline Riolo Guglielmo

"I came from a large family, and when I was in elementary school my mom cooked two hot meals almost every day. One of my favorites was Pasta Fagioli, (pasta and beans). I carried on this traditional dish with my own family. When my children were in college and asked for a hearty, inexpensive recipe to make, I would tell them to cook Pasta Fagioli. It's a simple, hot, and nutritional dish."

2 cans Cannellini Beans, (undrained)
1 8oz. can Tomato Sauce
½ pound Ditalini Pasta
1-1/2 cups water
2 Tablespoons Oil
½ small Onion (chopped)
Salt and Pepper to taste

In a 2-quart saucepan heat oil, sauté' chopped onion and garlic. Stir in tomato sauce and beans, then add water. Bring to slow boil and simmer for one hour and a half, stirring occasionally. Add more water if needed. (the secret to this is to simmer beans slowly).

Cook pasta al dente; Rinse and drain pasta, then stir into sauce mixture. Sprinkle with Pecorino Romano cheese and hot pepper flakes.

POTATO GNOCCHI

Kay Corpus

4 lb. potatoes
4 to 5 c. flour
1 beaten egg yolk
Salt to taste

Boil and mash potatoes. Gradually add flour. Knead until smooth, manageable dough is obtained. If needed, add more flour. Roll dough into long rope-like strips about 3/4 inch thick. Cut into 3/4 inch pieces and dip in flour. Use back of fork to make a dented design on each piece.

Boil in 8 quarts of salted boiling water for 10 minutes. Drain and serve with tomato sauce.

Serves 6 to 8.

RICOTTA GNOCCHI

Jennie Stromick

1 lb. Ricotta cheese
1 egg
1 tsp. salt
Flour as needed

Mix above ingredients with enough flour to make soft dough, and not too sticky. Roll dough into long rope-like strips about 3/4 inch thick. Cut into 3/4 inch pieces and dip in flour. Use back of fork to make dented design on each piece. Boil in 8 quarts of salted boiling water for 10 minutes. Drain and serve with tomato sauce.

SEAFOOD LASAGNA ROLLUPS

Marion Comito

6 lasagna noodles
1 (15-oz.) can tomato sauce

Filling:
1 (8-oz.) pkg. crabmeat (flakes or chunks)
¼ c. grated Parmesan cheese
1 egg
1 c. chopped shrimp (opt.)
1 T. dried parsley flakes
1 c. ricotta cheese
¼ tsp. onion powder

Cook noodles according to package directions. Rinse in cold water; drain well.

Filling: Thoroughly combine filling ingredients with fork. Spread ½ cup filling on each noodle. Roll tightly; place seam side down in a 9-inch square baking pan. Pour sauce over roll-ups.

Bake covered, in 375° oven for 30 minutes.

SHRIMP SCAMPI

Joan Panasci

1 Ib. shrimp
1 T. olive oil
1 T. butter or margarine
3 cloves minced garlic
2 T. chopped parsley
¼ c. white wine
¼ tsp. crushed red pepper

Melt butter in a large skillet. Blend in oil. When hot, add garlic and shrimp and sauté for 2 minutes until shrimp turns pink. Stir in all other ingredients and simmer another minute. Serve as an appetizer or over linguine.

WHITE CLAM SAUCE

Phyllis Kunigonis

1/4 c. olive oil
1 clove garlic, minced

Heat in skillet until garlic is lightly browned. Remove garlic and stir in slowly,

1/2 cup water
1/2 tsp. chopped parsley
1/4 tsp. oregano
1/2 tsp. Salt
1/4 tsp. pepper

Add 1 cup (8 ounce can) little neck clams, juice and all. Cook until clams are heated through. Serve hot on cooked spaghetti. If you prefer a red clam sauce, stir in 1 large can of tomato puree before adding clams and simmer about 30 minutes. Then add clams.

Marie Rotolo, Theresa Holmes, Sr. Mary Josita, & Johanna Carriero

PORK

• •

PORK CHOPS AND ORANGE SAUCE
••

Mrs. Jennie Jackson

¼ c. flour
1 tsp. salt
6 pork chops
1 Tbsp. oil
1 Tbsp. grated orange rinds
1 tsp. sugar
1 tsp. flour
½ c. water or orange juice
½ c. orange juice

Mix flour and salt together. Coat chops in this mixture and brown in oil in a heavy skillet. Poor off all the fat and then add orange juice to chops and cook slowly for ½ hour.

Remove pork chops from pan and keep hot in oven. Meanwhile, mix the orange rind, sugar, flour, water, and orange juice together until smooth. Stir into the skillet which chops were cooked and cook; stirring constantly until sauce is thick.

Pour over chops and serve.

PORK CHOPS WITH STUFFING
••

Beverly Zigrino

6 pork chops
10 slices white bread
1 small chopped onion
2 tsp. sage
1 egg
Salt and pepper

Place pork chops in baking dish. Mix stuffing. Moisten bread with water, squeeze and put in bowl; chop onion; add egg, sage and salt and pepper to taste. Mix well. Place 2 or 3 heaping tablespoons of stuffing on each pork chop. Place in oven; bake at 350° for 1 hour.

Suggested menu for above:
Pork chops with stuffing, Cranberry Sauce, Mashed potatoes, Green beans Favorite ice cream, Coffee - Tea - Milk

ZUCCHINI WITH HAM (Zucchini alia Romano)
••

Amy Breton

1 lb. zucchini
2 onions, peeled and chopped
1 clove garlic, crushed
Flour
Oil
½ lb. ham, cut into 4 pieces
½ c. grated Parmesan cheese
Salt and pepper

Cut zucchini into medium thick slices. Coat with flour, salt and pepper mixture. Heat a little oil in a skillet; add onion and garlic and cook until onion is soft. Add ham pieces and brown lightly. Remove ham and onion to a plate.

Heat a little more oil in the pan and place slices of zucchini in the pan. Allow just long enough for the zucchini to brown lightly. Arrange zucchini slices in a layer in a small baking dish; sprinkle with half the onion and half the grated cheese. Place the ham pieces on top of this and sprinkle with remaining onion and cheese. Top with the rest of the zucchini.

Place in moderate oven at 375°for about 15 to 20 minutes. Serve warm.

STEW

BEEF STEW WITH WINE

Mrs. Gloria Ceresoli

1 lb. stewing beef
Salt, pepper, and oregano to taste
1 small onion
1 c. red wine
1 clove garlic
2 Tbsp. tomato paste
2 Tbsp. oil

Cut beef in cubes. Brown onion and garlic in oil. Add beef and brown on both sides. Add salt, pepper, oregano and wine. Simmer until wine is reduced by half; stir in tomato paste and add hot water to cover meat.

Cover pot and simmer until beef is tender.

ZUCCHINI STEW

Mary Lanzi

"I have many good memories of homegrown zucchini. Every year my father planted zucchini in his garden and I would watch the plants grow into big beautiful "Googootz!" (slang in Italian). My mother was a wonderful cook who turned zucchini into delicious meals, including zucchini stew, zucchini frittatas, zucchini pancakes, zucchini parmesan, zucchini cutlets, zucchini bread and many more delicious creations. Ohooo, I can still smell and taste these wonderful dishes!" – MaryAnn Rotolo

1 whole onion
1 zucchini
2 potatoes
3 stalks celery
½ lb. Italian sausage
1 can string beans
(or fresh if you have them)
Salt and Pepper
Parsley
Oregano
Oil
8 oz. can Hunt's tomato sauce

Cut sausage into 1 inch pieces and brown in saucepan. Cut zucchini, potatoes and celery into good sized pieces. Flavor with salt, pepper, parsley and oregano. Pour a little oil over this mixture; add to the browned meat in saucepan. Add the Hunt's tomato sauce and 1 can of water. Let this cook until done (oil will rise to the top when stew is done). Last few minutes, add string beans and warm through.

Serve with crusty Italian bread. This stew may also be made without meat.

VEAL
• •

COTOLETTE ALLA CALBRESE (Veal Cutlets Calabrese)
. . . .
Lena Marcelletta

1½ lbs. veal cutlets
½ c. flour
2 egg yolks
1 c. bread crumbs
¼ c. butter or margarine
Lemon wedges
Salt & pepper

Gently pound the cutlets thin. Roll in flour. Beat egg yolks with salt and pepper. Dip the cutlets in the egg yolks and roll in bread crumbs.

Fry cutlets in the butter or margarine until golden brown.

Serve with lemon wedges.

Serves 4.

VEAL BIRDS
. . . .
Josephine Pasqualetti

12 very thin slices veal
12 slices Prosciutto or black pepper ham
2 eggs, slightly beaten
1 c. bread crumbs
½ c. water
1 lb. loose Italian sausage
Salt, Pepper, Garlic, Parsley to taste
1 c. dry white wine
1 c. meat stock or water

Veal should be very thin and about 4 inches square.

Mix sausage, bread crumbs, eggs, water and seasonings to make a stuffing mix. Place each slice of ham on top of each slice of veal. Put about 2 tablespoons of stuffing on top of ham, roll up ham and veal together and secure with toothpicks. Fry quickly in hot oil until nicely browned. Add wine and continue to simmer until wine evaporates. Add meat stock or water, cover and simmer until tender, about 1/2 hour.

Serve over rice with mushrooms if desired.

VEAL CHOPS WITH FETTUCCINE
. . . .
Gayle Bush

Veal chops
1 clove garlic
1 can chicken broth
Chopped parsley
¼ lb. butter or oleo

Fry veal chops with garlic until brown. Add 1 can chicken broth, chopped parsley and butter or oleo. Simmer covered for 20 minutes.

Cook fettuccine and pour meat juice over and serve.

VEAL CUTLET PARMESEAN

Mrs. Agnes Fontana

2 lbs. veal cutlet
2 eggs
1 c. breadcrumbs
½ c. oil
3 c. tomato sauce
Thinly sliced mozzarella cheese
Grated parmesan cheese

Heat oil in a large frying pan. Dip thinly sliced veal in beaten eggs and then in breadcrumbs. Fry in hot oil, until brown on both sides.

Place the brown cutlets in a shallow baking dish and place mozzarella cheese, sauce, and grated cheese on top.

Bake at 350° for 30 minutes.

VEAL PILLOWS

Lena Marcelletta

*"This veal dish is an easy, quick and delicious meal to serve any day of the week.
I made this frequently when my children were young. I will never forget the time my daughter, Annmarie, learned that veal came from a calf. Being an animal lover from a young age, she cried hysterically! It was then that she decided to become a vegetarian." – MaryAnn Rotolo*

12 small slices of veal cutlet (cut very thin in 4 inch squares)
12 small slices Prosciutto or ham, thinly sliced
12 thin slices Mozzarella cheese
2 Tbsp. butter
2 Tbsp. olive oil
½ c. Sauterne wine
1 tsp. butter
Salt and pepper to taste

Flatten out veal cutlet with a mallet or ask butcher to do it. Place one slice of Prosciutto or ham, and a thin slice of Mozzarella cheese on each cutlet and roll each cutlet using 2 or 3 toothpicks to hold together.

Melt butter in frying pan with oil heating same. Brown pillows well on all sides, turning each gently. They should be cooked in a short time.

Remove meat from pan; pour sauterne wine into it, scraping bottom and sides of pan well. Add 1 teaspoon butter, salt and pepper, heat and cook for a minute and pour sauce over pillows on serving dish.

Serves 6.

VEAL ROAST WITH PEAS

....

Mrs. Gloria Ceresoli

4 lb. veal leg or loin
4 cloves garlic
3 Tbsp. oil
Salt and pepper to taste
¾ c. white wine
2 c. peas

Pierce roast and place garlic in small holes. Put roast in roasting pan. Add oil, salt, pepper and wine. Cover pan and roast in oven (300°) for about 2 1/2 hours. Baste now and then. Add peas the last 1/2 hour.

Deacon Michael Gudaitis, Rev. Abraham "Fr. Abe" Esper, & Rev. Paul Angelicchio

Pizza & Sausage Bread

Marie Rossi

AUNT PEP'S EASTER MEAT PIE

Mary F. Lanzi

Crust:
6 c. flour
2 c. lard
1 tsp. salt
3 tsp. baking powder
1 c. cold water

Filling:
1 lb. Prosciutto
2 sticks Pepperoni
1 lb. basket of cheese
6 eggs, hard-boiled
12 eggs, well beaten
Black pepper to taste

Put dough at pan level. Roll out the top crust. Pour filling and cover with top crust, sealing well. Bake at 350° for 1 hour.

Cut prosciutto, pepperoni, basket cheese, and hard-boiled eggs into bite-size pieces. Mix together and add well-beaten eggs. Pour into crust, seal with top crust and bake at 350° for 1 hour.

FAMILY PIZZA DOUGH

Mrs. Sara R. Messineo

"My mother, Anna "Nunie" Stagliano, was a very close friend to Sara Messineo. I would have to believe they both used the same pizza dough recipe. They would share many conversations of their culinary skills. While in grade school, I remember arriving home, especially on Friday afternoons, to see a huge bowl covered with a special "moppina" (dish towel) sitting close to the heater. The bowl sat there to help the dough to rise. Once the dough had risen to my mother's liking, she turned it into the best homemade pizza pie ever! The next morning, maybe "pizza frittata" or maybe homemade bread! It was always a pleasant surprise to find out what creation my Mom would make with her famous homemade pizza dough!" - MaryAnn Rotolo

6 c. sifted flour
¾ c. lukewarm water
1 package dry yeast
2 tsp. salt
1 egg optional
2 Tbps. melted shortening

Dissolve yeast in water. Let's stand for five minutes.

In a large bowl, add 3 c. of flour and dissolved yeast with water. Mix well. Then add the remaining flour, melted shortening, and egg. Flour a breadboard and knead the dough for five minutes.

Place dough in a greased bowl and cover it with a damp towel. Let the dough rise for 1 ½ hour and then knead down.

Excellent for fried pizza or enough for two pizza pies.

PIZZA DOUGH AND SAUCE

Mrs. Agnes Fotana

1 lb. flour
1 tsp salt
1 c. lukewarm water
1 cake yeast
2 Tbsp. oil
2 c. tomato sauce
½ c. grated cheese

Dissolve yeast in lukewarm water. Sift flour and salt. Add yeast to the flour and knead thoroughly. Add oil and continue kneading until a smooth ball is obtained. Cover well and set aside in a warm place until the dough has raised to double in size.

When the dough is raised spread it on a large well-greased baking pan, about ½ to ¾ inches thick. Pour sauce on the dough and sprinkle generously with grated cheese. Add sliced mozzarella cheese, and pepperoni, sausage, or bacon. Bake in a hot oven for ½ an hour. Lower the temperature and bake for an additional 15 minutes.

PIZZA DOUGH

Joanne George

1 c. flour
1 tsp. salt
1 tsp. sugar
1 packet yeast
Shortening

Melt 1 small package of yeast in 1 ½ cups of warm water. Take two forkfuls of shortening and mash into the yeast mixture once the yeast is melted.

Mix all ingredients together in a bowl and make a hole in the center.

Pour the yeast mixture into the center of the flour mixture and slowly stir the center in from the sides. Spread (with hands) onto a plain or greased cookie sheet.

Let rise 1 to 2 hours. Bake 20 to 25 minutes at 450°.

SAUCE FOR PIZZA PIE

Mrs. Filomena Vito

1 qt. of tomatoes
1 pepper, sweet or hot
1 onion, chopped
3 garlic cloves, minced
½ stick of pepperoni
1 tsp. oregano
Pinch of salt

Fry the onion, garlic, pepper, and pepperoni in a saucepan with some famous brands of cooking oil. When this is cooked to one's taste, you can remove the onion and garlic, if you prefer. Add the tomatoes, salt, and oregano, to the oil and let cook for 1 ½ hour or more. If one desires you can use onion salt and garlic salt instead of the fresh flavor.

After the dough is pressed down on the cookie sheet, which has been spread with Crisco, you can spread the sauce over it. Bake the pizza in a preheated oven at 400° for about 15 minutes. Then add mozzarella cheese, and place back in the oven for another five minutes or until the cheese is melted or the bottom of the pizza is crisp.

SAUSAGE BREAD

Sue Rossi

Raw dough
Filling:
½ lb. loose sausage
1 egg
Mozzarella cheese
Grated cheese
Salt
Pepper
Onion salt
Garlic salt

Fry loose sausage; drain and let set.

Mix cooled sausage with one egg, grated Mozzarella cheese, grated cheese, salt, pepper, onion salt, and garlic salt.

Knead dough until thin. Spread the sausage mixture in the middle of the bread dough. Roll up like a jelly roll, closing sides and putting seam on the bottom.

Place roll in greased tin; rub the top with oil; bake at 400° for 30 to 35 minutes.

SAUSAGE ROLL

Patty Froio

1 pizza dough
1 beaten egg
½ lb. sweet sausage
½ lb. hot sausage
½ lb. shredded Provolone
or Mozzarella cheese
1 Tbsp. grated cheese
½ tsp. garlic powder
1 tsp. cooking oil

Take sausage out of the casing and break it into little pieces.

Add a little water to a frying pan and cook the sausage over medium heat.

Roll dough out in a round circle on a floured board. Spread beaten egg on top of the dough and add sausage pieces, shredded cheese, and grated cheese.

Roll the dough like a jelly roll and seal the ends. Rub oil on top of the roll and sprinkle with garlic powder. Bake in a pizza tin at 425 ° for 10 minutes.

Rosemary Giamporcaro marches with St John's in the Rome Honor America Days Parade

Sides

● ●

Rome Church's Confraternity, with Modest Beginning, Has Developed into Vital Part of Parish Social Life

Rome—A church society which started as nothing more than a plan for the religious training of high school pupils, but which has developed into a vital adjunct of the social life of the parish's younger set, is the Confraternity of Christian Doctrine of St. John the Baptist Church.

Currently comprising about 180 boys and girls of the parish, the confraternity, with headquarters in the church basement, arranges dances, games, hikes, athletic teams and otherwise caters to the recreational and social interests of the parish's younger set and its guests. And yet, while all this is more attractive to the average teen-ager, it is but incidental to the real purpose of the organization.

That purpose is the religious education of the high school student.

First organized in the parish by the late Rev. Edward O'Connell as part of a world-wide plan for religious education, the society was taken over in 1940 by the Rev. James Wolfe, who continues to be the guiding hand in its activities. Fresh out of North American College in Rome, Italy, Father Wolfe had enough young ideas to realize that to make a success of such a plan or training in religion completely successful, it needed extra incentive.

● ● ●

WITH THIS idea in mind, he launched the program of social and recreational activities which today marks an attractive side of the society. In the five years since the new curate took over, almost 2,000 members of St. John's parish have been members of the confraternity. So well was the ground work laid, that today Father Wolfe is able to let the organization practically run itself. Some of the activities which have made the confraternity a fixture in the parish are weekly dances, game nights and sport nights, with a couple of large scale annual dances thrown in for good measure. Hardly any of the local jive-music fans has forgotten the appearance last summer in Rome of Louis Armstrong at the YMCA. It was the confraternity that brought Armstrong to Rome. And it is now angling for another big name band to put in an ap-

Organizing the dances, game nights and other social activities of the Confraternity of St. John the Baptist Church, takes much planning and "over-the-table" work. Putting their heads together preparing the groundwork for a dance, are, from the left, Rinaldo Vera; Kenneth Pace, confraternity president; Jean Carnebianca, vicepresident; Gloria Pettinelli; and Leonardo Glasso. The tot is Gloria's brother, Johnnie, aged 3, who accompanied his sister.

pearance this summer.

Then, every Christmas, the society puts on a formal dance for its members and guests in Columbian Hall.

Its basketball team last year won the championship of the Rome Church League. The baseball team wearing the confraternity colors did not do as well. The organization also has its own monthly newspaper, a mimeographed job called the News-Record. The overall membership of the confraternity is composed of two large groups, leaders and students. The students, who are divided into 14 or 15 classes, all are of high school age, with the leaders past that stage of life.

● ● ●

THE STUDENTS chose their own class, as members of which they receive religious instruction from the leaders. These leaders, all of whom have been students in the confraternity, volunteer for their positions, and, after attending a summer school under Father Wolfe, are assigned a particular class.

Students select delegates, who,

with the leaders, compose a central council. This council maps all the activities of the entire organization.

The worth of the confraternity first made itself known during the hectic war years, when juvenile delinquency was rampant in the country. If there was one thing the young people of the United States needed at that time to keep them off the streets and out of trouble, it was organizations such as St. John's Confraternity.

● ● ●

BUT THE YOUTH of St. John's parish had such a club house on River St., to which they could adjourn nightly, thrash out topics of the moment, both religious and current, plan their activities, and, above all, stay out of trouble.

The first inkling which Father Wolfe received that his confraternity was contributing to the elimination of this great national sorespot was the appearance one morning a couple of years ago of a man, who told the priest he was from Washington, and was part of a committee making a study of the social problem.

As far as Father Wolfe

knows, no official report ever was published of the findings of this committee, but he does know that he received the commendation of the investigator on the "excellent work" of the Confraternity of St. John's.

● ● ●

That investigator probably did not realize, like many Romans, that the organization was formed for religious education, and not primarily for social life. But, if the two can mix, as they apparently can, it speaks well for the planning behind the scenes at 139 River St.

AUNT TILLIE'S RICE

Father Paul Angelicchio

½ c. cooked rice
½ c. chopped fresh mushrooms
½ c. chopped onion
½ c. cooked bacon
½ c. chopped celery
1 stick butter
3 large red sweet peppers, chopped

Melt butter in a pan; add mushrooms, onion, bacon, celery, and peppers. Simmer until cooked. Add cooked rice, and simmer until heated through.

Serves 4.

Makes a nice side dish for chicken.

BAKED BEANS

Mrs. Rose Lombino

1 lb. white beans
2 tsp. salt
½ c. sugar
1 large onion
1 small piece of salt pork or
¼ lb. of bacon

Soak beans overnight. Boil beans, salt, sugar, onion, and salt pork or bacon until tender.

Pour mixture into baking dish and bake for 1 hour at 350°.

CORN FRITTER

Mrs. Louise Carissimo

1 ¾ c. flower
3 tsp. baking powder
1 ½ tsp. salt
1 slightly beaten egg
1 c. milk
1 Tbsp. melted shortening
½ c. home-cooked or canned
whole-kernel corn

Sift flour, baking powder, and salt. Combine beaten egg, milk, and melted shortening, and then pour into flowered mixture and stir until smooth. Add corn.

Place spoon-sized mixture into deep hot fat at 365°to 375°, and fry for 3 to 5 minutes or until well browned on all sides.

Make sure to turn the fritters as they rise to the surface.

Drain on absorbent paper.

*Makes about six servings. Can be served with hot syrup

ESCAROLE AND BEANS

Amalia Fusco

4 lb. escarole (or dandelion)
1 clove garlic
¼ c. oil
Salt and pepper
(hot pepper if desired)
1 can white beans

Wash escarole thoroughly. Place in a large pan; cover with water. Boil until tender, about 15 minutes. Drain.

In a 4 quart saucepan, fry the garlic in oil until light brown. Remove pan from heat and add escarole. Simmer for 15 minutes. Pour beans over escarole.

With 2 forks gently turn until mixed. Add salt and pepper, cover, and cook over low heat for another 20 minutes. Add a small amount of water if the liquid boils down.

Best if made early in the day, so the flavor will blend.

ITALIAN CAULIFLOWER

Virginia Pisano

1 medium size head cauliflower
1 Tbsp. olive oil
¼ c. bread crumbs
¼ c. grated cheese
¼ c. olive oil

Wash and clean cauliflower. Break into flowerets. Cook in a small amount of boiling salted water, until half done, about 6 minutes. Drain.

Grease bottom of a baking pan with 1 tablespoon of olive oil and arrange cauliflower on the bottom.

Combine crumbs and cheese. Sprinkle over flowerets. Season with pepper. Drizzle 1/4 cup olive oil on top.

Bake in 350° oven for 30 minutes.

*If becomes dry, add ¼ cup water.

POTATO PANCAKES

Mrs. Rose Swerediuk

6 medium-sized potatoes
¼ tsp. baking powder
1 egg
4 level Tbsp. flour
1 level Tbsp. butter
Salt and pepper to taste

Peel potatoes and grate on the small side of the vegetable grater. After the potatoes are grated, add other ingredients and mix them together. On a hot skillet, put two heaping tablespoons of mixture onto the skillet and let brown on both sides.

Serve warm with cottage cheese or just plain.

*Serves approximately four

RICE MELANAISE
....

Barbara Amoroso

"My wonderful mother-in-law, Angie Amoroso, shared this delicious recipe with me and I think of her whenever I make it, which is quite often."

½ stick butter – I use unsalted
1 small onion chopped
1 c. raw rice – no Minute Rice
2 chicken bouillon cubes
2 c. water
½ c. dry white wine
2 Tbsp. chopped Italian flat-leaf parsley
1 Tbsp garlic powder
¼ c. grated pecorino romano or parmesan cheese

Bring the above ingredients to a slow boil, lower the heat to simmer, and cover for 20 minutes.

If dry, add some water.

SAUSAGE STUFFING
....

Fil Manuele

½ c. butter or margarine, melted
1½ c. chopped onion
1 c. chopped celery stalks with leaves
1 Ib. sausage meat, browned and drained
1 tsp. poultry seasoning
2 T. fresh parsley, chopped
1 tsp. salt
½ tsp. pepper
1 c. turkey or chicken stock
1 egg, slightly beaten
8 c. day-old bread, cubed

Melt butter in a large skillet, add onion and celery and sauté until tender. Add browned sausage. Toss to combine.

Remove from heat and add to bread cubes. Add seasonings, stock, and beaten egg. Mix well.

SCALLOPED POTATOES
....

A Friend

½ c. flour
½ tsp. salt
1 large can of College Inn chicken plain broth
paprika

Place butter, or oleo, flour, and salt and make into paste form and add chicken broth. Bring to a boil.

Pour over sliced potatoes in a deep casserole and sprinkle with paprika.

Bake at 325° for ½ hour.

SWEET POTATO CROQUETTES

Mrs. Bambina Schillaci

"I never had the pleasure of tasting Bambina's croquettes, but I can tell you about a funny story about my friend "Bam". One day, on a snowy winter day, I decided to go to the Rome Savings Bank on E. Dominick St. where I ran into Bam. She and I had once worked together, and Bam was a long-time friend to my family, so naturally, we wanted to catch up. We had a very nice conversation and then went about our business. When I returned home, I got a call from Bam, and she was laughing hysterically. She told me she had decided to check something in her oven before she left her house and had thrown a "moppina" (dish towel) around the collar of her winter coat. She said, "Oh my goodness, why didn't you tell me I had a moppin' around my neck? Oh dear! The teller must've thought I lost my mind!" I told her I didn't think anything about it -- I thought she was using it as a scarf! That was one of many comical moments and good times with this wonderful, humorous, loving lady."
- MaryAnn Rotolo

3 c. sweet, potatoes, mashed
¼ c. butter
1 tsp. salt
2 tsp. brown sugar
½ tsp. cinnamon
½ Tbsp. nutmeg
½ c. crushed pineapple, drained
1 egg

Combine all ingredients and shape into balls about 1 ½ inches in diameter.

Beat an egg slightly with a fork. Roll the balls in the egg and then roll them in breadcrumbs.

Add 1 tsp. water and prepare fine, dry bread, or cracker crumbs. Dip balls in crumbs, then dip in a beaten egg and return to the crumb mixture again.

Fry in hot fat at 375° to 385° until brown. Drain on absorbent paper.

Msgr. Cicciarelli, Kristi Maggio & Grandma Salerno (1977)

Sauces

· ·

CHICKEN BARBECUE SAUCE

Viola Ermenio

1 pt. vinegar
1 egg
3 Tbsp. Kraft barbecue sauce
2 tsp. salt
1 tsp. pepper
2 tsp. poultry seasoning

Mix ingredients all together.

Makes a little less than a quart of sauce.

CHICKEN BARBEQUE SAUCE

Mrs. R. Dursi

½ pt. oil
1 pt. vinegar
3 Tbsp. salt
½ tsp. pepper
2 tsp. poultry seasoning
1 egg

Combine all the above ingredients to make a barbeque sauce.

Halve or cut up 5 chickens and marinate overnight. While the chicken is cooking on the outdoor grill, continue to baste with sauce. Turn chicken several times for even cooking.

Makes enough sauce for 10 halves of chicken.

*If becomes dry, add ¼ cup water.

ITALIAN BARBECUE SAUCE

Delcie Castro

¼ c. oil
2 cloves garlic, minced
2 chopped onions
1 (29 oz.) can puree
2 Tbsp. wine vinegar
2 Tbsp. brown sugar Pinch of salt
1 tsp. pepper
¼ tsp. oregano

Heat oil in a saucepan. Add garlic, and onion and saute lightly. Stir in the remaining ingredients.

Simmer for 30 minutes.

ITALIAN SAUCE FOR SPAGHETTI

Miss Rose Lambino

1 lb. sausage
1 lb. hamburger
2 garlic cloves
¼ c. oil
1 2 oz. can tomatoes
1 can paste
salt and pepper to taste
1 bay leaf
2 eggs
1 c. grated cheese
¼ c. Italian cheese
1 sprig of parsley

Boil 1 clove of garlic, tomatoes, paste, and bay leaf for 1 ½ hour.

Fry sausage until brown and add to sauce

In a large bowl, add hamburger, eggs, grated cheese, Italian cheese, one garlic clove, parsley, and salt and pepper to taste. Mix meatball ingredients together and roll into round balls. Fry in deep fat. Then add to sauce and cook for another ½ hour for flavor.

RHUBARB SAUCE

Ollie Tyler

4 c. rhubarb
1 box wild strawberry jello
2 ½ c. sugar

Slice rhubarb thin and add sugar. Let stand in a bowl for 1 hour.

Then boil rapidly for 5 minutes.

Remove from heat and scatter the jello on top and mix thoroughly.

Put in jars, seal with wax or you may keep it in the refrigerator for 3 or 4 weeks.

Wild cherry jello may be substituted and is equally as good.

Pickles & Relishes

· ·

Elizabeth Voci

PICKLES

BREAD AND BUTTER PICKLES

Mrs. Nettie Volpe

8 c. cucumbers
2 c. onions
4 green peppers
4 red peppers
2 c. vinegar
2 tsp. celery seed
2 tsp. turmeric seed
3 tsp. mustard seed
3 c. brown or white sugar
salt

Slice pickles, onions, and peppers salt them and soak overnight. Then heat vinegar and sugar with spices then add cucumbers. Let the mixture come to a boil and cook for an additional 20 minutes.

Fill pickles in jars and seal them.

DILL PICKLES

Mrs. Jenny M. Vaccaro

4 c. water
1 c. vinegar
½ c. salt
8 sprigs of dill
1 garlic clove

Mix vinegar, water, and salt well. Heat mixture to boiling point. Place pickles in jars. Add the dill sprigs and garlic.

Pour hot mixture into jars of Pickles and seal. Allow to set for several weeks.

DILL PICKLES

Mrs. Joseph Squallace

Cucumbers
3 cloves of garlic
3 dill greens
1 c. white vinegar
2 Tbsp. salt
1 c. water

Wash cucumbers and pack in jars with garlic, dills, and water.

Bring to boil; pour over pickles and seal at once.

Makes 2 quarts.

ZUCCHINI PICKLES

....

Ollie Tyler

2 lb. zucchini, cut into thin slices
¼ c. salt
1 tsp. celery seed
1 tsp. turmeric
2 small onions, cut into thin slices
2 c. white vinegar
2 c. sugar
2 Tbsp. mustard seed

Cover zucchini and onions with salt and water. Let stand for 2 hours and drain.

Bring the remaining ingredients to a boil and pour over the vegetables. Let stand for 2 hours. Bring to a boil for 5 minutes. Pack in sterilized jars.

Makes 3 pints.

PICKLED VEGETABLES

PICKLED EGGPLANT

Carol Mosca Ceci

1 qt. screw-top jar
1 small eggplant (about 1 lb.)
⅔ c. wine vinegar
4 cloves garlic, quartered
2 hot peppers, chopped
(or 1 tsp. Ground red pepper)
½ tsp. minced onion (or dry)
Pinch oregano
Olive oil (or any good oil)

Wash and slice eggplant thin; slice in two again. Layer in a jar; add garlic and pepper between layers. Set aside.

Combine wine vinegar, oregano, and onions and pour the mixture over eggplant. Add enough oil to cover the eggplant.

Top jar and store in the refrigerator for a few days.

Serve cold.

PICKLED GREEN TOMATOES

Mrs. John Parker

2 qt. sliced green tomatoes
3 Tbsp. salt
2 c. vinegar
⅔ c. brown sugar
1 c. granulated sugar
3 Tbsp. mustard seed
½ tsp. celery seed
1 tsp. turmeric
3 c. sliced onions
2 sweet peppers, sliced
1 hot pepper, sliced

Mix tomatoes and salt and allow to stand for at least 12 hours or overnight. Drain. Heat vinegar, sugars, and spices to boiling point. Then add onions and boil for about 8 minutes. Add tomatoes and peppers; bring to boiling point again and simmer for 5 minutes more, stirring occasionally. Pack in hot sterile jars. Seal immediately.

Makes 2 quarts.

PICKLED VEGETABLES

Sue Ferlo

Glass canning jars
Peppers
Onions
Cauliflower
Cherry peppers (hot or sweet)
Wine vinegar or cider vinegar
Water
Salt

Wash and cut up peppers, onions, and cauliflower. Mix 1 gallon of vinegar with ¾ gallon of water and 5 teaspoons of salt. Alternate vinegar mixture with vegetables, filling canning jars, making sure no air bubbles remain in the jar. Seal and set in a cool place.

Do not move for 2 weeks. You will find the best results if you place the vinegar mixture in a large open container and stir as you use it.

RELISH

● ●

CRANBERRY ORANGE RELISH
....
Mrs. Filament Vito

4 c. (1 pd.) ocean spray fresh
cranberries
2 oranges, quartered
(remove seeds)
2 c. sugar

Put cranberries and oranges (including rind) through a food chopper. Add sugar. Chill. Keep in refrigerator for weeks. This is very good with chicken, turkey, or other meats.

You can also make cranberry orange relish salad by making raspberry-flavored gelatin (following the directions on the package, but using 1 ½ cups instead of 2). When the mixture begins to gel, fold in 1 c. cranberry orange relish. Pour into mold and chill until firm.

When ready to serve unmold and decorate with fresh cranberries and springs of parsley.

Makes two pints.

Desserts

• •

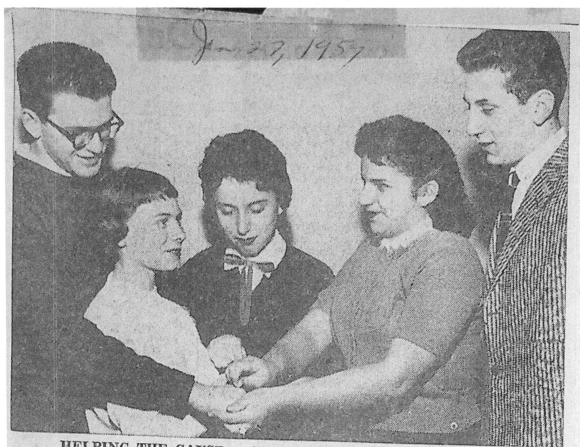

HELPING THE CAUSE — Among the 250 youngsters who attended the polio dance at St. John the Baptist Church social hall last night were the above teenagers who are being "stamped" for admission. Left to right they are Sal F. Comito, 16, son of Mr. and Mrs. Emanuel Comito, 123 Third St.; Susan J. Doolittle, 15, daughter of Mr. and Mrs. Howard N. Doolittle, Yorkshire Apartments; Mary E. Ross, 15, daughter of Mr. and Mrs. Joseph J. Ross, 151 River St., co-chairman of dance; Patricia A. Taverna, 17, daughter of Mr. and Mrs. Joseph D. Taverna, 111 Kossuth St., dance chairman, and Joseph A. Tosti, 17, son of Mr. and Mrs. Philip E. Tosti, 104 Third St., president of the Confraternity of St. John's, which sponsored the dance. Proceeds will be added to the polio fund. The following mothers made pizza which was served: Mrs. Tosti, Mrs. Henry Bush, Mrs. Peter Belmont and Mrs. Rose Bottini. The Rev. Nicholas R. Maio, confraternity moderator, was present.

CAKE

APPLE COFFEE CAKE

Angela Tallarino

3 c. flour
2 c. sugar
2 tsp. baking powder
1 c. oil
4 eggs
½ c. orange juice
2 tsp. vanilla
4 apples
2 tsp, cinnamon
5 Tbsp. sugar

Cut apples into thin slices; mix with cinnamon and sugar (set aside). Blend remaining ingredients and beat until smooth.

Grease a tube pan and pour half of the cake mixture in the pan and then add apples evenly around; pour the rest of the batter over the apples.

Bake at 350° for 1 ½ hours.

APPLE UPSIDE DOWN CAKE

Mary Fahey

"I remember helping my mom, Julia Strange, with this Apple Upside Down Cake. It was her mother's recipe. I would be peeling the apples as she would be cooking the syrup on the stove. The smell in the house was heavenly. She would serve it warm with homemade whipped cream. It was one of my father's favorite desserts."

¼ cup spry (you can use oil too)
¼ tsp. of each: salt, cinnamon, nutmeg, allspice
1 cup sugar
1 egg beaten
2 ½ cups sifted flour
3 tsp. baking powder
1 cup milk
4 cups sliced apples

Syrup:
6 T. spry + 1 T butter, firmly packed
4 T. milk
1 cup brown sugar
1 cup sugar

Grease 9X13 pan. Line bottom with wax paper. Put sliced apple in bottom and drizzle with syrup mixture. Spoon batter on top.

Bake °350 45 min.

QUICK APPLE CAKE
....
Mamie Guggi

2 c. apples, sliced
1 c. sugar
1 egg, well beaten
1/4 c. salad oil
1 c. flour
1 tsp. cinnamon

1 tsp. baking soda
¼ tsp. salt
½ c. raisins
½ c. chopped nuts

Put apples in a bowl; add sugar, oil, eggs, and mix. Add remaining ingredients. Bake in loaf pan at 350° for 45 minutes.

BANANA CAKE
....
Frances Spadafora

1 box yellow or white cake mix
2 eggs
½ c. water
1 tsp. baking soda
¼ c. oil
1 c. ripe mashed bananas

Mix together cake mix, 1 egg, water and baking soda. Blend well. Now add bananas, 1 egg, and oil. Beat together.

Bake at 350°.

BEER SPICE CAKE
....
Carolyn R. Franco

½ c. butter
1 c. brown sugar
1 egg, lightly beaten
1 ½ c. flour, sifted
1 tsp. baking powder
1 tsp. cloves
1 tsp. cinnamon

1 tsp. allspice
¼ tsp. baking soda
¼ tsp. salt
1 c. nuts, chopped
1 c. dates, chopped
1 c. beer

Cream together butter and brown sugar until mixture is light and fluffy. Stir in egg.

Sift together flour, spices, baking soda, and salt. Then sift dry ingredients over chopped nuts and dates and add this mixture to butter mixture alternately with beer.

Butter a loaf pan ad pour in mixture. Bake at 375° for 30 minutes, or turn pour into muffin tins and bake for 20 minutes.

BOILED RAISIN CAKE

Theresa Pristera

In a large bowl:
1 c. Crisco
3 eggs
1½ c. sugar

Stir. Add:
1 tsp. salt
1 tsp. cinnamon
1 tsp. baking soda
1 tsp. nutmeg
3 heaping tsp. baking powder
1 tsp. ginger
Cherry juice from jar of cherries
1 tsp. cloves

Boil 1 package (15 ounces) raisins with 3½ cups water for 15 minutes (1 cup of water should be left with the boiled raisins).

Pour in boiled raisins with water. Stir. Start adding flour (from 4½ to 5 cups). Before all flour is added, add in a cup or more of walnuts and chop in the cherries. Stir well until shiny. You can decorate top with walnut halves and cherries. Grease Bundt pan very well. Bakes over 1½ hours as it is a big cake.

Bake at 350°; watch for burning.

CANNOLI CHEESECAKE

Anna Anania

1 (3-1b.) ctn. (6 c.) whole milk ricotta cheese
7 lg. eggs
1¼ c. granulated sugar
½ c. all-purpose flour
1 T. vanilla extract
1½ c. semi-sweet chocolate mini chips

Topping:
3 T. apricot preserves, melted
3 sm. navel oranges, peeled and white pith cut off, then thinly sliced
¼ c. shelled pistachio nuts, skins rubbed off

Heat oven to 350°. Lightly grease and flour an 8-inch spring-form pan.
Tap out excess flour. Wrap outside of pan with heavy-duty foil, molding it tightly around pan to prevent water from seeping in. Process ricotta cheese in food processor, scraping down sides once or twice until completely smooth. In a large bowl whisk eggs, sugar, flour, vanilla and grated orange peel until blended. Stir in ricotta until blended and smooth.

Pour batter in prepared pan and spread evenly. Sprinkle chocolate chips over top. Place pan in a large roasting pan in oven. Pour hot tap water to a depth of 1 inch into roasting pan. Bake 1½ hours or until top is golden and cake pulls away slightly from sides of pan (middle will still jiggle slightly when pressed lightly). Turn off heat and prop open the oven door about 1 inch. Let cake cool in oven for about 45 minutes.

Remove from oven, then remove foil. Cool completely on wire rack. Cover and refrigerate overnight or up to 1 week. Up to 3 hours before serving, run a thin long knife around edge of pan to loosen cake. Remove sides of pan. Brush top of cake with half of the melted preserves. Top with layer or orange slices and brush with remaining preserves.

CARROT CAKE

....

Barbara Ann Dibble

1 c. sugar	Frosting:
1 c. sifted flour	1 to 3 c. sugar
½ c. vegetable oil	1 Tbsp. margarine or butter
1 egg	3 drops maple flavoring
Dash of salt	⅓ c. evaporated milk
1 tsp. cinnamon	Chopped walnuts
¾ tsp. baking soda	Dash of salt
¾ tsp. baking powder	
¼ c. ground walnut meats	
1 jar strained babj' carrots	

Mix ingredients in large bowl and pour into a 5 x 9 inch greased baking pan. Bake in preheated oven at 350° for about 25 minutes.

Mix ingredients and spread on cake when cool. Sprinkle chopped walnuts on top.

CARROT CAKE

....

Sally Mungari

3 c. flour	Frosting:
2 c. sugar	¼ c. butter
2 tsp. baiting powder	1 oz. cream cheese
2 tsp. baking soda	2 c. confectioners sugar
1/2 tsp. salt	1 tsp. vanilla
1 tsp. cinnamon	
1 ¼ c. oil (vegetable)	
1 tsp. vanilla	
1 c. grated carrots	
½ c. walnuts	
½ c. raisins	
1 egg	

Put all dry ingredients in one bowl and add your liquids and mix real well; add carrots, nuts and raisins last. Bake at 350° for 1 ½ hours.

Cream together until smooth and add on top of cake.

CHEESE CAKE

Mary F. Lanzi

1 lb. cream cheese
¼ lb. butter
1 lb. Ricotta cheese
1 pt. sour cream
4 eggs
3 Tbsp. vanilla
3 Tbsp. lemon juice
1 ½ c. sugar
3 Tbsp cornstarch
3 Tbsp flour
Graham Crackers

Butter a 9 inch spring form pan and sprinkle with graham cracker crumbs. Beat cream cheese and butter at high speed. Add and beat Ricotta; add and beat sour cream.

In another bowl beat eggs, vanilla, and lemon juice; add to cheese mixture and beat.

In another bowl mix sugar, cornstarch and flour; blend into above mixture.

Bake at 350° for 1 hour. Turn off oven, do not open it. Leave cake in oven for another hour.

Remove from oven; cool completely before removing from spring form pan.

CHEESE CAKE CRUST

Ange Tallarino

1 ½ c. crushed graham crackers
¼ c. melted butter
¼ c. sugar

CHOCOLATE CAKE

Mrs. Joseph Capponi

¾ c. shortening
1 c. buttermilk
1 ½ c. sugar
2 eggs
2 c. flour

1 tsp. vanilla
½ c. cocoa
2 tsp. baking soda
½ c. warm water

Mix all ingredients together. Bake at 375° for 40 minutes.

CHOCOLATE CHIP CAKE
....

Author Unknown

1 c. chopped dates	1 ¾ c. flour
1 ½ c. boiling water	¾ tsp. baking soda
1 ½ tsp. baking soda	½ small package chocolate
¾ c. shortening	chips
1 c. sugar	¼ c. sugar
2 eggs, unbeaten	1 c. nuts

Pre-heat oven to 350 degrees for 45 minutes

Combine first 3 ingredients and let stand until cool. Do this about 1 hour ahead of time to make sure the mixture is thoroughly cooled.

Grease a 12 by 9-inch pan and lightly flour the bottom. Cream shortening and sugar at a high speed on mixer. Add egg and continue beating at high speed until mixed well. Add date mixture. Add soda, flour, and salt into batter. Use low speed when adding flour. Mix until well-blended and pour into pan. For topping, sprinkle chocolate chips evenly over top and make sure to get chips to the edges of the pan. Then sprinkle sugar over top, then chopped nuts. Bake at 350°.

Make this cake in this order as listed as chocolate chips may burn if put in last. May be served with whipped cream or vanilla ice cream.

CHOCOLATE FROSTING
....

Mrs. Henry Baptiste

1 sq. melted chocolate	⅓ c. evaporated milk	Put all ingredients in a bowl and beat with a mixed
½ c. granulated sugar	¼ tsp. salt	master or blender until fluffy.
⅔ c. shortening	1 tsp. vanilla	
1 Tbsp cold water		

CHOCOLATE OIL CAKE
....

Sue Rossi

¾ c. oil	2 c. flour	Mix all ingredients in order listed above. Bake at 350°
1 ¼ c. sugar	1 tsp. baking powder	for 30 minutes or less.
1 egg	2 tsp. baking soda	
1 tsp. vanilla	1 c. boiling water	Frosting:
¾ c. cocoa		1 envelope Dream Whip
¾ c. milk		1 ½ c. milk
		1 box instant pudding (vanilla or chocolate)

Blend ingredients and frost.

CLASSIC BACARDI RUM CAKE

Jean Ceci

1 c. chopped pecans or walnuts
1 (18½-oz.) pkg. yellow cake mix
1 (3¾-oz.) pkg. Jello vanilla instant pudding and pie filling
4 eggs
½ c. cold water
½ c. oil
½ c. Bacardi rum

Glaze:
¼ lb. butter
1 c. sugar
¼ c. water
½ c. rum

Preheat oven to 325° and flour 10-inch or 12-inch bundt pan. Sprinkle nuts over the bottom of the pan. Mix all cake ingredients together. Pour batter over nuts. Bake for 1 hour. Cool.

Melt butter in a saucepan. Stir in water and sugar. Boil for 5 minutes stirring constantly. Remove from heat. Stir in rum.

Invert the cake on a serving plate. Prick the top and drizzle and the glaze evenly over the top and sides. Allow the cake to absorb the glaze. Repeat until the glaze is used up.

COCONUT CREAM POUND CAKE

Mary F. Lanzi

3 c. flour
1 tsp. baking powder
½ tsp. salt
3 c. sugar
3 sticks butter or oleo
¾ c. Crisco
½ tsp. coconut extract

1 ½ tsp. vanilla extract
1 c. milk
5 large eggs
1 c. flaked coconut

Let eggs stand at room temperature for 1 hour before using. Meanwhile, butter and lightly flour a large Bundt cake pan and heat the oven to 325°.

In a large bowl blend butter, shortening, and flour mixture on low speed. Then add coconut and vanilla extracts. Now, still at low speed alternately add milk and eggs, one at a time, beating well after each addition; fold in coconut.

Pour into the pan and bake at 325° for about 1 hour and 10 minutes or until a cake tester comes out clean. Cool on wire rack for 10 minutes. Slice when cool.

CRANBERRY SAUCE CAKE

Jenny Guggi

3 c. flour
1 c. sugar
1 tsp. baking soda
1 tsp. salt
1 can cranberry sauce
1 c. walnuts

1 c. Hellmann's
mayonnaise
1 orange rind
½ c. orange juice

Sift all dry ingredients, then add mayonnaise, orange rind, and orange juice. Mix well; add walnuts and cranberry sauce. Pour in a 9-inch layer or loaf pan.

Bake at 350° for 1 ¼ hour

Frosting:
¼ c. cranberry sauce
1 c. Jack Frost sugar
2 Tbsp. margarine

Blend ingredients and spread when the cake cools.

CREAM CHEESE POUND CAKE

Mary F. Lanzi

1 (8 oz.) pkg. cream cheese
1 ½ c. sugar
4 eggs
1 ½ c. flour
¾ c. chopped nuts
½ lb. oleo
1 ½ tsp. baking powder
1 ½ tsp. vanilla
1 c. candied fruit (cherries and pineapple)

Blend soft cheese, oleo, sugar, and vanilla. Add eggs, one at a time, beating well after each egg. Gradually add 2 cups of flour with baking powder. Combine other ½ cup flour with fruit and nuts and fold into batter.

Grease and flour tube pan; sprinkle with grated nuts, and pour cake batter into pan.

Bake at 325° for 1 hour and 20 minutes.

CREAMY FROSTING

Mrs. Sue Aquino

2 Tbsp. flour
1/2 cup milk

Cook until a paste forms and let cool. Make sure it is very cool.

Combine:
¼ c. butter
¼ c. shortening
½ c. granulated sugar

Add the above cream mixture to paste, then add:

1 tsp vanilla
2 tbsp confectioners sugar

Then whip until it looks like cream.

DARK DEVIL'S FOOD CAKE

Mrs. Millie Raulli

2 ¼ c. sifted cake flour
1 ¾ c. sugar
⅓ tsp. double acting baking powder
1 ¾ tsp. baking soda
1 tsp. salt
⅔ c. cocoa
⅔ c. high-grade shortening
⅔ c. water
1 ½ or ⅔ c. unbeaten eggs

Sift flour, baking soda, baking powder, and salt. Mix in shortening and water. Beat vigorously with a spoon for two minutes by the clock, or with electric mixer, on medium speed for two minutes.

Add eggs. Beat two more minutes. Pour into prepared pans pan size, 9 x by 1 ½ inches or oblong 13 x 9 ½ by 2 inches. Bake at 350° for 30 minutes; for layers bake 30 to 40 minutes.

Cool and frost with your own favorite frosting or use this one:

½ c. shortening
½ tsp. salt
¼ c. milk
2 Tbsp. cake flour
¾ box sifted confectioners sugar
1 tsp. vanilla

Beat ingredients together until it looks like whipped cream. Then frost your cake or cupcakes. In fact, this is good on your cookies, too.

DR. BIRD CAKE

Florence Laurie

3 c. flour
1 tsp. baking powder
1 c. granulated sugar
1 ½ c. oil
1 c. crushed pineapple (do not drain)

1 ½ tsp. vanilla
3 eggs
1 c. diced bananas
½ c. chopped nuts (optional)

Mix all ingredients in order of appearance. Bake in a greased bundt or tube pan in a medium oven at 350° for approximately 1 hour and 20 minutes.

Powdered sugar may be sprinkled over the cake before serving.

**This cake is excellent for freezing.

DUTCH APPLE CAKE

Mrs. Mary R. Inglund

2 c. pastry flour
½ tsp. salt
3 tsp. baking powder
¼ c. of shortening
½ c. sugar
1 egg

⅔ c. milk
1 tsp. vanilla
2 Tbsp. melted butter
3 apples, sliced thin
4 Tbsp. sugar
1 tsp. cinnamon

Sift and then measure flour. Sift again with salt and baking powder.

Cream the butter; add sugar, egg, milk, and vanilla. Add flour to the butter mixture.

Pour into greased pan and press apples into the batter.

Sprinkle the sugar and cinnamon over top. Bake at 400° for 30 to 35 minutes.

FOOL'S CHOCOLATE DELIGHT CAKE

Mrs. Helen Natale

½ c. cocoa
½ c. cold water
2 tsp. baking soda
½ c. shortening
1 ¾ c. sugar
2 egg yolks
1 c. milk
2 ½ c. flour
1 tsp. vanilla
1 tsp. baking powder
2 egg whites

Mix cocoa, cold water, and baking soda. Let stand then cream with shortening, sugar, and egg yolks. Beat until smooth.

Mix baking powder and flour. Alternatively, add milk and flour mixture to creamed mixture. Mix thoroughly.

Beat egg whites until stiff and fold into mixture. Add vanilla.

Place in a greased pan. Bake at 350° for 45 minutes.

E-Z COFFEE CAKE

A. Guaspari

1 can Pillsbury country-style biscuits
(not buttermilk)
Sugar
cinnamon
1/4 c. sugar
1/2 stick oleo or butter

Place sugar and cinnamon in a plastic bag. Cut biscuits in quarters. Place quarters in the bag and shake. Place quarters in 8-inch cake tin or pie tin. Melt and boil together.

Blend ¼ c. sugar and butter and spread over biscuits.

Bake at 350° for approximately 45 minutes.

FESTIVE CAKE

....

Josephine Bird

3 c. flour, sifted
2 c. sugar, granulated
1 tsp. salt
1 tsp. cinnamon
2 eggs
1 ½ c. oil
1 tsp. almond extract
1 c. bananas
1 (8 oz.) can crushed pineapple
1 c. chopped almonds

Mix and sift flour, sugar, baking soda, salt, and cinnamon; stir in almonds.

Beat eggs slightly; combine with oil, almond extract, bananas, and undrained pineapple.

Add to dry ingredients; mix thoroughly, but DO NOT BEAT. Spoon into a well-oiled 10-inch tube pan.

Bake at 325° for 1 hour and 20 to 25 minutes.

Cream Cheese Frosting for Festive Cake:
1 box confectioners sugar
½ c. butter
1 (8 oz.) pkg. cream cheese

Blend all ingredients until creamy. Invert the cake on a rack and cool before frosting.

Makes 12 to 16 servings.

FRENCH CHOCOLATE CAKE

....

Josephine Calandra

4 sq. chocolate
1 c. boiling water
1 egg
2 tsp. baking soda
2 tsp. vanilla
2 c. flour
1 c. sugar
½ c. buttermilk (or 1/2 c.sour milk)
1 tsp. salt
½ c. butter

Place chocolate, butter, and sugar in a bowl; add boiled water and stir until sugar and butter are dissolved. Add baking soda; stir in buttermilk, eggs, and vanilla; add flour sifted with salt and beat.

Pour in well greased layer pans. Bake at 375° for 30 minutes.

Frosting:

1 box confectioners sugar
4 sq. melted chocolate
¼ c. oleo
1 tsp. vanilla
¼ c. warm milk

Put confectioners sugar and butter in a bowl; add milk until the right consistency. Add vanilla and chocolate; mix well. More milk makes it creamier and darker.

FRUIT CAKE

. . . .

Mrs. Mary Lombino

"Living in East Rome (now called "Little Italy"), we were blessed to have a Concord grape vine, red and yellow apple trees, and a mint bush in our backyard. Rose Lombino was our next-door neighbor. It was a given, during the Fall season, that I'd see her picking apples, grapes, and herbs out of our backyard. Once she felt she had enough fruit she would go back to her home to start baking her prize pies and desserts. It was a given she would always return with a pie to share with our family. To this day, the memory still warms my heart as much as that warm pie warmed my stomach." – MaryAnn Rotolo

1 cup melted shortening
1 1/2 cups sugar
2 eggs
1 lb raisin
3 1/2 cups water
3 cups flour
1 tsp baking soda
1 tsp baking powder
1 tsp vanilla
1 cup chopped walnuts
2 tsp cinnamon
1 tsp allspice
1 cup assorted gumdrops,
cut in small pieces

If desired, trim top with 1/2 cup walnuts. Take the water and raisins and boil them for 5 minutes and let this cool. Sift flour once, measure, add baking powder, baking soda, cinnamon, and allspice, and sift together 3 times.

Melt shortening and cool. Add sugar and eggs and vanilla and cream together. Add flour and alternate mixing with water and raisins. Add chopped nuts and gumdrops. Baked in 10x10x 2 inch pan. Bake at 375° for 45 minutes.

FRUIT CAKE

. . . .

Josephine S. Taverna

½ lb. shortening
2 lbs. seedless raisins
2 c. water
3 c. sugar
3 eggs
2 c. chopped nuts
2 tsp. baking soda
1 tsp. salt

1 tsp. Cinnamon
1 tsp. Cloves
1 tsp. Allspice
Small can of fruit cocktail
5 c. flour

Boil raisins, water, and sugar for five minutes. Let cool; add shortening. Gradually add all other ingredients. Stir until well-mixed. Bake in greased tins at 350° until cake tester comes out clean.

Makes 8-10 pounds. Freezes well.

GENOISE CAKE WITH PEACHES

Mary McGowan

6 eggs
1 c. sugar
½ tsp. salt
½ tsp. vanilla
1 c. sifted flour
½ c. melted butter
1 c. frozen or fresh peaches
(strawberries may be substituted)
¼ c. confectioners sugar
1 c. heavy cream

Beat the eggs until thick and lemon colored. Gradually add sugar and beat until fluffy. Add salt and vanilla (beating time: 10 minutes).

Fold in the sifted cake flour. Fold in melted butter.

Pour into 2 greased and floured layer cake pans and bake at 350° for 30 minutes. When the cakes are cool, slice and add whipped cream and peaches or berries.

Refrigerate for 2 hours before serving.

HARVEY WALLBANGER SUPREME CAKE

Theresa Sergio

1 pkg. Duncan Hines orange
supreme cake mix
1 (3 ¾ oz.) pkg. vanilla instant
pudding mix
½ c. Crisco oil
4 oz. frozen orange juice
4 oz. water
4 eggs
3 oz. Galliano
1 oz. vodka

Blend all ingredients in a large bowl; beat for 5 minutes.

Pour into greased and floured 10-inch tube pan and bake at 350° for 45 to 55 minutes or until the center springs back when touched lightly.

Cool in pan for about 15 minutes.

Glaze:
1 c. confectioners sugar
1 Tbsp. orange juice
1 ½ Tbsp. Galliano
1 Tbsp. vodka

Blend confectioners sugar, orange juice, Galliano, and vodka. Spread over the cake while warm.

HOLIDAY WONDER CAKE (FRUITCAKE)

Mrs. Helen Natale

1 c. sugar
½ c. shortening
1 egg
1 c. chopped nuts
½ c. raisins
1 tsp. cinnamon
½ c. mixed citrus fruit
½ c. dates

1 tsp. allspice
1 tsp. cloves
1 tsp. baking soda
1 tsp. baking powder
2 tsp. nutmeg
1 c. sour milk
2 ½ c. flour

Cream shortening and sugar. Add egg and beat in milk, baking soda, powder, and flour until smooth. Then add spices, nuts, raisins, dates, and citrus fruit, each separately.

Place mixture into a greased 10-inch pan and bake at 350° for approximately 1 hour.

ITALIAN SPONGE CAKE

Rita Troncone

6 eggs
1 ½ c. sugar
1 Tbsp. orange juice
Pinch salt
1 ½ c. flour

Beat eggs fast for 15 minutes; add sugar a little at a time.

Beat again for 15 minutes. Add 6 tablespoons of orange juice.

Beat at Number 1; add flour and beat for just a few minutes.

Preheat the oven to 325° and bake for 45 minutes.

JEWISH COFFEE CAKE

Luguinia Curcio

1/4 lb. oleo (1 stick)
2 c. flour
1 c. sugar
1 egg
1 tsp. baking powder
1 tsp. baking soda
1 tsp. vanilla
1 c. sour cream (commercial)

Mix all ingredients. Pour half of the batter in a greased tube pan and sprinkle with half of the following mixture:

¼ c. sugar
1 tsp. cinnamon
½ c. chopped nutmeats

Pour remaining batter on top and sprinkle rest of the sugar mixture.
Bake for 35 minutes at 375°.

JIFFY'S DEVIL FOOD CAKE

Mrs. Henry Baptise

1 ½ c. sifted flour
1 c. sugar
3 Tbsp. cocoa
1 tsp baking soda
½ tsp. salt
½ c. melted shortening or cooking oil
1 tsp. vanilla
1 tsp. vinegar
1 c. cold water

Sift flour, sugar, cocoa, baking soda, and salt. Sift again.

Make 3 depressions in the flour mixture. Pour melted shortening in one depression, vinegar in the second, and vanilla into third. Pour cold water over all the mixture and beat until blended. The batter should be very thin.

Bake at 350° for 30 minutes.

*This is a dark soft cake.

JO'S SPONGE CAKE DELIGHT

Mrs. Josephine Agone

1 ½ c. cake flour
1 c. sugar
½ tsp. baking powder
¼ tsp. salt
5 egg yolks
1 ½ c. sugar
1 Tbsp. lemon juice
½ c. cold water
¾ tsp. cream of tartar

Sift the cake flour, baking powder, and salt. Resift five times.

Beat egg yolk and ½ c. of sugar. Slowly add lemon juice and cold water until it is light and lemon colored.

Stir the flour mixture into three parts with ⅓ of the liquid ingredients. Beat five egg whites until foamy; add cream of tartar. Beat until the egg whites are stiff (but not dry) and fold them into the flour mixture.

Bake in a 10-inch tube pan at 325° for 60 minutes.

For a filled sponge cake:

18 oz. crushed pineapple
1 c. shredded coconut
20 diced marshmallows
12 or more maraschino cherries
1 c. whipped heavy cream
vanilla

Hollow the cake leaving a 1-inch shell and use a piece of the top crust to fill the hole in the bottom. Shred the removed cake and combine it with crushed pineapple, shredded coconut, marshmallows, maraschino cherries, and whipped heavy cream.

Fill the ingredients inside the shell. Cover the top with heavy cream whipped, to which you may add vanilla for flavoring.

Chill for eight hours before serving.

LUCY'S CAKE
....
Marie Angelicchio

4 eggs
1 tsp. baking powder
1 c. sugar
1 tsp. vanilla

1 c. flour
1 c. raisins
¼ tsp. salt
½ to 2 c. chopped nuts

Beat eggs until very stiff and frothy; gradually add sugar. Measure and sift dry ingredients. Blend well into egg and sugar mixture; add vanilla, raisins, and chopped nuts. Bake at 350° in 12 x 8-inch pan for 30 to 35 minutes.

MARASCHINO CHERRY CAKE
....
Mrs. Dorothy Bauer

2 c. plus 2 tsp. cake flour
3 tsp. baking powder
1 ⅓ c. of sugar
½ tsp salt
1 ½ c. shortening
1 ½ c. milk
1 5 oz. five bottle maraschino cherries and juice
5 egg whites
1 c. chopped nuts

Mixed flour, baking powder, salt, and sugar. Then add shortening, milk, maraschino cherries and juice, and beat for 2 minutes. Add egg whites and chop nuts.

Place in 2 greased nine-inch cake pans. Bake at 350° for 30 to 35 minutes.

Cool and frost.

MARASCHINO PARTY CAKE
....
Mrs. Sue Aquino

2 ¼ c. sifted cake flour
1 ⅓ c. sugar
3 tsp baking powder
1 tsp salt
½ c. shortening
¼ c. maraschino cherry juice
16 maraschino cherries, cut in eighths
½ c. milk
4 large egg whites, unbeaten
½ c. chopped nuts, if desired

Preheat oven to 350°. Grease and flour two 8-inch cake pans. Sift flour, sugar, baking powder, and salt together. Add shortening, cherry juice, cherries, and milk. Add egg whites, then add nuts.

Bake for 30 to 35 minutes.

OATMEAL CAKE

Jo Ann Lloyd

1 ½ c. boiling water
1 c. oatmeal
½ c. oleo
1 c. brown sugar
1 c. white sugar
½ c. nuts
1 tsp. soda
½ tsp. baking powder
1 ½ c. flour
1 ½ tsp. cinnamon

Mix oatmeal, oleo, brown and white sugar, and boiling water. Allow oatmeal mixture to cool. Add nuts, baking soda and powder to cooled oatmeal. Mix in flour and cinnamon.

Bake at 350° for 35 to 45 minutes in a 13x9 inch pan.

ORANGE CRANBERRY CAKE

Jessie Ilodkinson

Prepare:

1 c. dried dates
Rinds or 2 oranges (chopped in small pieces)
1 c. chopped walnuts
1 c. fresh cranberries (whole)
1 c. sugar
¾ c. salad oil
1 c. milk
1 tsp. vinegar
Add:

1 ¼ c. flour
1 tsp. baking powder
1 tsp. salt
1 tsp. baking soda

In a large bowl, mix 2 eggs, well beaten. Add: sugar, oil, milk and vinegar. Next, blend in flour, baking powder, salt, and baking soda. Add prepared fruits.

Pour in a greased tube pan and bake at 350° for 1 hour.

Refrigerate 24 hours before cutting.

*Make frosting before refrigerating with ¾ cup orange juice and ¾ cup sugar.

PEACH UPSIDE DOWN CAKE

Mrs. Katherine Kane

Melt in a baking pan:

2 Tbsp. shortening
⅓ c. brown sugar

Arrange peaches on top of this mixture.

1 c. white sugar
⅓ c. shortening
½ tsp. salt
1 teaspoon vanilla
1 ½ c. flour
2 tsp. baking powder
1 c. milk
1 egg combine
⅓ c. shortening
salt
vanilla

Combine shortening, salt, and vanilla. Add sugar in gradually.

Cream until fluffy. Beat in egg. Stir the flour and baking powder. Add milk to the flour and blend in well with the above mixture. Pour over peaches.

Bake at 350° for 35 to 40 minutes.

Loosen the edges and turn over on a server platter.

PINEAPPLE ICEBOX CAKE

Sue Rossi

2 eggs
½ c. pineapple juice
¼ tsp. salt
½ c. sugar
Vanilla wafers
1 Tbsp, gelatin (soaked in 1/4 c. water)
1 c. crushed pineapple
1 c. cream
Pecans

Separate eggs. Make a custard with beaten egg yolks, sugar, salt, and pineapple juice. Add soaked gelatin to hot custard and cool.

Fold in crushed pineapple, beaten egg whites, and whipped cream.

Fill a buttered 9x9 inch dish with layers of vanilla wafers and the pineapple mixture. Top with crushed wafers and pecans.

Chill thoroughly. Keep in the freezer until ready to serve.

PINEAPPLE UPSIDE DOWN CAKE

Mrs. Sue Aquino

⅓ c. Spry
¼ tsp salt
1 tsp vanilla
½ c. sugar
1 egg, unbeaten
1 ½ tsp. baking powder
1 ¼ c. sifted flour
½ c. canned pineapple juice
½ c. brown sugar, firmly packed
5 slices canned pineapple
5 maraschino cherries, optional

Combine Spry, salt and vanilla. Add sugar gradually and cream well. Add egg and beat thoroughly. Add baking powder to flour and sift 3 times. Add small amounts of flour to cream mixture, alternately with pineapple juice, mixing after each addition until smooth.

Sprinkle brown sugar on the bottom of a 8 x 8 inch pan rubbed liberally with Spry. Arrange pineapple on sugar, with cherries in the center of slices, and pour batter over all.

Bake at 350° for 50 to 60 minutes.

Serve upside down with whipped cream.

Serves 8 to 10.

PISTACHIO CAKE

Mary Milanoski

1 pkg. white cake mix
1 pkg. pistachio pudding
½ c. oil
½ c. milk
½ c. water
5 eggs

Blend cake mix with pudding mix. Add oil, milk, and water. Add eggs, one at a time, beating well after each addition.

Pour into a greased Bundt cake pan; bake at 350° for 1 hour.

PISTACHIO CAKE FROSTING

Eleanor Ferlo

½ pt. heavy cream
1 pkg. instant pistachio pudding
1 small container of Cool Whip

Beat cream until thick. Blend pudding and Cool Whip into cream and spread on cake.

POOR MAN'S CAKE

Concetta Marechioni

1 c. water
1 c. sugar
1 c. Mazola oil (or an.v kind)
1 box raisins
1 tsp. cloves
2 tsp. cinnamon

½ tsp. Ginger
1 tsp. baking soda
½ tsp. Salt
1 c. nuts
4 c. sifted flour

Mix water, sugar, oil, raisins, cloves, cinnamon, and ginger. Then add flour, baking soda, salt, and nuts.

Bake at 300° for 30 minutes or more. Check with a cake tester.

POUND CAKE

Viola Ermenio

2 sticks butter
6 eggs
2 c. sugar
1 c. flour
½ pt. whipping cream
1 tsp. vanilla

Cream butter and sugar. Add cream, eggs, and flour alternately, beating well after each addition. Stir in flavoring.

Bake at 325° for 1 to 1 ½ hours in a tube pan. Cool and remove from the pan.

Sprinkle top with confectioners sugar.

PUMPKIN CAKE

Ange Tallarino

3 c. flour
2 c. pumpkin
2 tsp. baking powder
2 tsp. baking soda
½ tsp. salt
1 c. oil
1 c. sugar
1 egg
½ tsp. cinnamon
1 cup nuts
1 cup chocolate chips

Mix all ingredients together and add nuts and chocolate chips.

Grease and flour a tube pan. Bake at 350° for 1 hour and 15 minutes.

POLISH NUT ROLL

Mrs. Dominick Marchione

Sweet Dough:

1 c. warm milk
2 eggs
½ c. sugar
½ c. shortening
1 pkg. dry yeast, diluted with 1/4 c. warm milk
Pinch salt
4 c. flour

Mix dry ingredients in a bowl; make a well in the center and add diluted yeast. Mix with hands and cover with a piece of clean cloth or dish towel and let rise until double. When it rises, divide the dough into 4 pieces and spread it on a floured board. Put ¼ of the filling over the dough and roll.

Filling:
1 lb. ground nuts
¾ c. warm milk
1 tsp. cinnamon
2 c. sugar

Mix well and divide into 4 parts. Spread over the dough with a butter knife and roll like a jelly roll. Baste the top of the nut rolls with a beaten egg yolk.

Bake on a greased cookie sheet at 350° until golden brown.

QUEEN ELIZABETH CAKE

Ange Amoroso

1 c. boiling water
1 c. chopped dates
1 tsp. baking soda
1 c. sugar
¼ c. butter
1 beaten egg
1 tsp. vanilla
1 ½ c. sifted flour
1 tsp. baking powder
½ tsp. salt
½ c. nuts

Pour boiling water over chopped dates and baking soda. Let stand. Cream together sugar and butter. Add egg, baking powder, vanilla, salt, flour, and nuts.

Bake at 350° for 35 minutes.

Icing:

1 Tbsp. brown sugar
2 Tbsp. butter
1 Tbsp. cream (milk)

Boil for 3 minutes; spread on hot cake; sprinkle with coconut or nuts.

RICE CAKE

Clara Boiko

1 egg
1 ½ c. Ricotta cheese
1 ½ c. sugar
½ c. milk
1 ½ tsp. cinnamon
5 c. cooked rice

Beat eggs and sugar together for 1 ½ minutes. Mash cheese slightly and mix with milk and cinnamon. Add to egg mixture and stir in rice.

Pour into a buttered 8x8 inch square baking dish. Bake at 350° for about 1 hour. You may add orange peel and lemon peel also.

RICOTTA-FILLED MARBLE POUND CAKE

Eleanor Ferlo

Filling:

3 lb. fine Ricotta
1 c. confectioners sugar
1 c. maraschino cherry juice
½ c. maraschino cherries, cut up
1 small chocolate-almond bars
1 carton heavy cream

Beat Ricotta until smooth; add sugar and cherry juice and continue beating. Fold in cherries and grated chocolate bars.

Cut 2 loaves of marble pound cake in ⅛ inch slices and place in a large round cake pan, 3 inches deep or use a deep oblong pan. Alternate layers of cake with filling.

Let stand overnight.

Tip the cake pan over on the serving dish and cover with whipped cream.

SOUR CREAM BLUEBERRY CAKE

Elaine Gorski

½ c. soft oleo
1 c. sugar
3 eggs
2 c. flour
1 tsp. baking powder
1 tsp. soda
1/2 tsp. salt
1 c. dairy sour cream
1 tsp. vanilla
2 c. blueberries
½ c. brown sugar

Cream oleo and sugar. Add 3 eggs, one at a time; beat well after each.

Sift flour, baking powder, soda, and salt. Add sour cream.

Mix vanilla, blueberries, and brown sugar. Fold in 1 cup of the berry mixture and pour half the batter into a well-greased and floured 9 x 13-inch pan. Cover with remaining berries mixture. Sprinkle with brown sugar.

Bake at 350° for 45 to 50 minutes.

Cool in pan for 10 minutes. Remove to rack to finish. Check after 30 minutes.

SOUR CREAM CAKE

Jacqueline Baynes

¼ lb. butter
1 c. sugar
3 eggs
1 c. flour
1 tsp. baking powder
1 scant tsp. baking soda
1 c. sour cream
1 tsp. vanilla
½ c. semi-sweet chocolate
(Nestle's)
½ c. brown sugar
½ c. chopped nuts

Grease a 10-inch tube pan and heat over to 350°.

Cream butter and sugar until fluffy; add eggs, flour, baking powder, soda; add alternately with sour cream; stir in vanilla and chocolate chips.

Topping: Combine brown sugar and nuts and a little cinnamon. Sprinkle over batter.

Bake for 45 to 50 minutes.

SUNSHINE CAKE

Margo Taylor

"This cake recipe was given to me by a dear friend and co-worker back in 1989. It was our favorite for celebrating birthdays."

1 box Yellow Cake Mix
½ c oil
1 mandarin orange, small can, juice and all
4 eggs

Mix all ingredients together on low for 30 seconds until incorporated. Then mix on med-high for 2 minutes until thick. Pour into greased and floured 9x12 pan. Bake at 325° for 45 minutes or until the center springs back when you touch it.

Frosting:

1 Cool Whip, medium
1 crushed pineapple 15 oz, juice and all
1 box Vanilla Instant Pudding, small

Beat together until firm. Frost the cake when completely cooled. Refrigerate after frosting.

SUPERB COFFEE CAKE

Chris Bart

¾ c. sifted cake flour
1 ½ tsp. baking powder
½ tsp. baking soda
½ pt. sour cream

Topping:
¼ c. granulated sugar
½ c. raisins
1 tsp. vanilla
½ c. shortening
¾ c. granulated sugar
1 egg, unbeaten
2 tsp. cinnamon
½ c. chopped walnuts

Heating at 350°. Grease 9-inch spring form pan with tube insert in place, or a 9 x 9 x 2-inch pan.

Sift flour, baking powder, and soda. In a large bowl, mix shortening with sugar and eggs until light and fluffy. Then, with a mixer at low speed, beat in flour, sour cream, and vanilla.

Turn half of the batter into the pan. Sprinkle half of the topping over the batter and top with the rest of the batter, and follow again with the remaining topping; press lightly with spoon.

Bake for 45 minutes or until done. Serves 9 to 12.

WALNUT CROWN POUND CAKE

Mary F. Lanzi

1 c. chopped walnut meats
1 ¾ c. flour
1 ¾ c. sugar
1 ¼ tsp. baking powder
1 tsp. salt
¾ c. milk
1 c. oleo or butter
1 tsp. vanilla

Grease and flour a 9 or 10-inch Angel cake pan. Spread walnut meats over the bottom.

Sift dry ingredients together in a large mixing bowl. Add milk, oleo, and vanilla. Beat for 2 minutes, scraping bowl frequently.

Add the unbeaten eggs. Beat 2 minutes more. Pour over walnut meats in the pan.

Bake at 375° for 50 to 60 minutes.

Walnut meats form topping. Needs no icing.

WATERGATE CAKE

....

Joey Cicconi California

1 box yellow cake mix
1 box Pistachio instant pudding
3 eggs
1 c. Club soda
1 c. oil (Wesson or Crisco)
½ c. chopped nuts (optional)

Mix all ingredients for about 4 minutes.

Grease and flour a 9 x 13 bundt cake pan.

Pour batter into pan and bake at 350° for 55 to 60 minutes.

Icing:

2 envelopes Dream Whip
1 c. cold milk
1 box Pistachio instant pudding

Beat all together until thick and spread on cake.

CANDY

• •

CARAMEL CHEWS
• • • • • • • • • • • • • • • • • • • •

Lorraine Rossi

28 Kraft caramels
1 Tbsp. margarine
1 Tbsp. water
3 (3 oz.) can chow mein noodles
2 c. peanuts
1 (6 oz.) pkg. semi-sweet chocolate bits
2 Tbsp. water

Melt caramels with margarine and water in a saucepan over low heat. Stir occasionally until the sauce is smooth.

Add noodles and peanuts. Toss until well coated.

Drop by rounded teaspoonfuls onto greased cookie sheet.

Melt chocolate pieces with water in a saucepan over low heat. Top chews with melted chocolate mixture; chill until firm.

Makes 2 ½ dozen.

CHOCOLATE CREAMS
• •

Rosemary Maio

2 lb. confectioners sugar
1 can condensed milk
¼ lb. butter or oleo, melted

Mix all ingredients well. Add a few drops of milk if too stiff.

Divide into bowls and add flavorings and "extras" - maple with nuts, almond with cherries, coconut, vanilla, orange, rum, etc.
Form into balls (if necessary, chill first) and chill for 1 hour.
Dip in chocolate as with peanut butter candy (see recipe).

SESAME SEED AND HONEY CANDY

Jean Ferlo

1 lb. sesame seed
2 Tbsp. water
1 c. honey
1 c. blanched almonds

Prepare seeds by washing them through a strainer and then set them in an aluminum pie tin. Blanch almonds and sliver (cut), and place in another pie tin.

Place in oven at 200° for ½ hour. Set aside.

Heat sugar and water on low heat, stirring constantly. When the mixture starts to boil and darken (color of honey), add honey, sesame seeds, and almonds. Cook over low heat until the mixture is sticky and leave the side of the pan, stirring constantly (approximately 15 minutes).

Lightly grease a Pyrex pan or aluminum square pan and spread in the mixture.

While hot, sprinkle nonpareils candies.

Cool and serve.

COOKIES

● ●

"My grandmother would make trays of cookies for friends and family. If any cookies were not perfect, they couldn't go on the trays. She made us eat them!" - Kathy Loreto

ANISE COOKIE STICKS

Virginia Pisano

½ c. butter
1 (3 oz.) pkg. cream cheese
1 c. sugar
1 c. flour
3 tsp. baking powder
½ tsp. salt
2 tsp. anise seed

Cream butter and cream cheese together. Gradually add sugar, creaming thoroughly after each addition. Beat in eggs, one at a time, and continue beating until light and fluffy. Add a mixture of remaining ingredients; mix well.

Divide dough in half; place on a lightly greased cookie sheet and form into 2 rolls the length of a baking sheet and 1 ½ inches wide.

Bake at 350° for 30 to 35 minutes or until light brown.

Remove from oven and cut rolls crosswise into slices about ¾ inch thick.

Place on baking sheet cut side down. Return to oven and bake 10 minutes longer or until toasted and crisp.

ALMOND CUT COOKIES

Mrs. Inessa Darkangelo

12 well-beaten eggs
1 lb. sugar
1 lb. melted spry
5 tsp. baking powder
5 tsp. almond flavoring
3 lb. flour

Beat eggs well. Add sugar, melted spray, dry ingredients, and almond flavor.

Mix well and roll into one inch thickness and the length of the baking sheet. Place the rolls on a greased cookie sheet (about five to a sheet) and bake at 350° until a delicate brown.

Remove from oven and let cool.

Then cut cookies at an angle, about one inch wide, and place back in the oven cut side up for 10 minutes.

ALMOND COOKIES

Mrs. Mary Mosca

3 egg whites, beaten
1 lb. confectionery sugar
1 lb. almond paste
1 tsp. baking powder

Mix ingredients with an electric mixer.

Shape into small balls. Add half a maraschino cherry on top of the balls. Place on a greased cookie sheet.

Bake at 370° for 15 minutes.

ALMOND DELIGHTS

Gloria Lynne Ceresoli

5 lb. almond paste
3 lb. confectioners sugar
1 dozen egg whites (stiff)
Dried cherries or Pogneli nuts

Break up paste and mix with sugar; add stiff egg whites; let stand for 1 hour.

Rub hands with shortening; roll into balls the size of a walnut; place on a greased cookie sheet; decorate with pieces of cherries and Pogneli nuts.

Bake at 350° for 20 to 30 minutes, or until they are light brown.

Remove almond delights from the cookie sheet as soon as they come from the oven to prevent sticking.

BISCOTTI

Mal Clemente

¾ c. oil
¾ c. sugar
3 eggs, beaten
3 c. flour, sifted
2 tsp. anise, vanilla or almond flavor
½ c. almonds or walnuts, chopped
2 tsp. baking powder

Beat oil, sugar, and eggs. Then and remaining ingredients. Let set before putting onto a greased cookie sheet.

Form 3 logs 1½ inches wide.

Bake 350° for 20 minutes.

Slice and put back in oven for 10 minutes for toasting.

BOURBON BALLS

Virginia Pisano

2 1/2 c. crushed vanilla wafers
1 c. confectioners sugar
1 Tbsp, cocoa
1 c. finely chopped nuts
1 Tbsp, corn syrup
¼ c. bourbon (rum, brandy, whiskey may be substituted)

Mix the first 4 ingredients. Add syrup and bourbon; mix well. Roll into 1-inch balls and roll in sifted confectioners sugar.

Place in a tight container.

Yield: 3 1/2 dozen.

BOURBON BALLS

Mrs. Mary Selvetti

2 ½ c. crushed vanilla wafers
1 c. confectioners sugar
2 Tbsp. cocoa
1 c. nuts, finely chopped
2 Tbsp corn syrup
¼ c. bourbon (rum, Brandy, or whiskey may be substituted)

Mix the first four ingredients. Add syrup and bourbon. Mix well. Roll into one-inch balls and roll in sifted confectioners sugar. Place in a tight container. Will keep indefinitely.

Yields 3 ½ dozen.

"My Aunt Jennie made these often. I can still see her standing by the stove frying them in the cast iron frying pan. The best part is sprinkling on the confectioners sugar." – Patti Martinelli

BOW TIES

Mrs. Nettie Volpe

6 egg yolks
2 Tbsp. heavy cream
Pinch salt
One small glass of whiskey
Flour

Cream egg yolks until smooth. Add salt, heavy cream, and whiskey. While mixing add enough flour to make a soft dough.

Roll into thin strips, about 1-inch wide and six inches long. Tie into a bowl and fry in hot fat until brown.

When cool sprinkle confectionery sugar on top.

CHERRY COOKIES

Angeline Gualtieri

1 c. Spry
1 c. sugar
4 eggs
1 c. milk
1 c. flour
4 tsp. baking powder
Pinch salt
2 tsp. almond extract
Red food coloring
1 c. chopped cherries

Mix all ingredients together with enough flour to roll.

Shape into small round balls and bake at 400° for 12 to 15 minutes. Cool and frost.

CHERRY-PISTACHIO BISCOTTI

Patricia DeProspero

2 c. all-purpose flour
1 c. sugar
2 tsp. finely grated lime peel
1 tsp. baking powder

¾ c. dried tart cherries
3 large eggs, beaten with a fork
1¼ c. shelled, lightly salted pistachio nuts
½ stick (¼ c.) cold butter, cut into small pieces

Heat oven to 350°. Lightly grease a large cookie sheet.

In a food processor, process flour, sugar, lime peel, and baking powder until blended. Add butter and cherries. Pulse until cherries are coarsely chopped. Spoon off and reserve 1 tablespoon of the beaten eggs. Add the remaining eggs and the pistachios to the food processor and pulse until dough is evenly moistened.

Turn dough out on a well-floured work surface (dough is sticky). Divide dough into quarters. With hands, roll each portion into a 9-inch log. Place logs crosswise 3 inches apart on prepared baking sheet. Press logs to flatten to 2 inches wide. Brush with reserved egg.

Bake for 25 minutes or until golden brown. Let cool on a sheet on a wire rack for 10 minutes. Loosen with a spatula and remove to a cutting board. Let cool 10 minutes longer.

Using a large heavy knife, cut each log diagonally in ½ inch thick slices. Arrange slices upright on a clean cookie sheet (no need to grease sheet) and bake 14 to 16 minutes longer until crisp. Remove to wire rack to cool (cookies will get even crispier).

CHEWY NOELS

Josephine Grasso

2 eggs, beaten
1 c. brown sugar
5 Tbsp, flour
½ tsp. soda
1 tsp. vanilla
1 c. chopped nuts
2 Tbsp. melted butter
Sugar

Mix ingredients together. In an 8x8-inch pan, add 2 tablespoons of melted butter and nuts. Pour the mixture over the nuts and butter.

Bake at 400° for 30 minutes.

Cut in squares and roll in sugar.

"I have very vivid memories of my aunts, Mary and Rose, making cookies for weddings by the bushel. As a kid, with my brother and sisters, we would also help mom with the cookies at Christmas. We were all young but each had a job chopping nuts and cherries, grinding figs, or frosting."- Patti Martinelli

CHOCOLATE COOKIES (FOR WEDDINGS OR PARTIES)

Mrs. Dorothy Bauer

5 lb. flour
1 ½ lb. sugar
1 ½ lb. shortening
3 tsp. baking powder
3 tsp. vanilla
6 eggs, well beaten

1 qt. milk
1 tsp. cloves
1 tsp. cinnamon
1 lb. peanuts
1 lb. cocoa
chocolate chips

Mix the dry ingredients. Then add wet ingredients.

Form into small balls.

Bake at 350° for 15 minutes. Cool and frost.

CHOCOLATE COOKIES

Author unknown

1 large c. oil
1 large c. sugar
pinch of salt
2 Tbsp. baking powder
1 package chocolate chips
⅓ c. nuts
⅓ c. cocoa
1 c. milk
Flour to make hard dough

Combine ingredients, drop on cookie sheet.

Bake at 400 degrees for 15-20 minutes.

CHOCOLATE CHIP & PEANUT BUTTER COOKIES

Sr. Mary Elise

2½ c. flour
1 c. peanut butter
½ tsp. salt
1 c. white sugar
½ tsp. baking soda
1 c. brown sugar
1 c. margarine
2 eggs

Mix flour, salt and baking soda; set aside. Mix margarine and peanut butter. Add both kinds of sugar; mix well. Add eggs; beat well.

Stir flour mixture into peanut butter mixture.

Drop dough from teaspoon on baking pan.

Flatten with fork. Bake at 375° for 10-15 minutes.

CHOCOLATE MEATBALLS

Jennie Sanzone

1 c. shortening
1 c. milk
8 oz. cream cheese
1 tsp. vanilla
½ c. flour
5 tsp. baking powder
½ c. cocoa

½ tsp. cinnamon
¼ tsp. cloves
¼ tsp. nutmeg
1 ¼ c. sugar
½ c. nutmeats
1 c. chocolate chips

In a large bowl, add ingredients all together and mix well. Make a soft dough and refrigerate for 1 hour or overnight.

Make little balls the size of walnuts. Bake at 375° for 15 minutes.

Make a soft icing of powdered sugar, milk, and dip cookies while still warm.

CHOCOLATE REFRESHERS

Angela Tallarino

1 ¼ c. flour
½ tsp. salt
¾ tsp. baking soda
1 ½ c. (8 oz.) cut dates
½ c. butter
¾ c. brown sugar
½ c. water
½ c. orange juice
½ c. milk
1 c. chopped walnuts

Sift flour, salt, and baking soda. Set aside. In a large saucepan, cook dates, butter, brown sugar, and water, stirring constantly until dates soften. Remove from heat. Stir in 1 cup chocolate chips; add 2 unbeaten eggs; mix well. Add dry ingredients alternately with orange juice and milk.

Blend thoroughly. Stir in walnuts. Spread batter on a well-greased pan (cookie sheet).

Bake at 350° for 25 to 30 minutes.

Cool and frost.

Makes about 3 dozen bars.

CHERRY COOKIES

Mrs. Mary Lumbino

1 c. shortening
4 eggs
2 c. sugar
1 tsp. vanilla
2 or 3 tsp. almond flavoring
1 c. milk
5 tsp. baking powder
8-ounce cherries, cut up
½ chopped nuts (optional)
2 lb. flour
red food coloring

Mic shortening and sugar together. Add eggs and half of milk, baking powder, coloring, almond, and vanilla. Add the remainder of milk and enough flour to form a soft dough.

Add cherries and nuts. Shape into small balls and place two inches apart on a baking sheet. Bake at 375 ° for 12 minutes. Frost with butter frosting, using almond flavoring.

*Makes about 87 cookies.

COCONUT MACAROONS

Nancy Marcello

½ c. (about ½ can) sweetened condensed milk
1 tsp. vanilla extract
¾ tsp. almond extract
1⅔/ c. (two 3½-oz. cans or Ig. 7 or 8-oz. pkg.) flaked coconut

Combine all ingredients in a bowl; mix until well blended. Drop by teaspoonful about 1 inch apart on a well-greased cookie sheet. Bake in a moderate oven (350°) for 8-10 minutes. Makes about 1½ to 2 dozen cookies. Top each cookie with half a cherry or walnut before baking.

"My mother baked tons of Christmas cookies that my sisters and I reluctantly had to Frost!" - Mary Natalie

CHRISTMAS COOKIES

Mrs. Mary Mosca

2 ½ lb. mixed chopped nuts
1 lb. raisins
1 lb. pineapple
1 ½ c. honey
1 Tbsp. almond flavoring
2 c. flour

Mix ingredients together and shape into small round loaves. Wrap in tin foil and place on a cookie sheet. Bake at 350° for one hour. Cool and cut into slices.

"One of my favorite Christmas memories is of my Mom baking dozens of different kinds of Italian Christmas cookies! She loved solitude while baking but I was allowed to frost the cookies sometimes. My Dad would be sitting on the couch watching TV and often ask her if she had any "mistakes" he needed to eat!!"
– Annette Marullo

CHRISTMAS ROSES
....
Mrs. Mary Mosca

½ qt. white wine
½ qt. cooking oil
½ lb. sugar
2 lb. flour
3 tsp. baking powder
1 lb. walnuts
1 lb. almonds
1 lb. raisins
honey

Mix ingredients together. Roll out as you would a pie crust into sheets ¼ inch thick.

Mix walnuts, almonds, and raisins. Use enough, honey to hold the filling together.

Spread filling on sheets of dough. Then roll as you would a jelly roll and brush with cooking oil. Cut rolls into pieces of 6-inches.

Grease the cookie sheet. Bake at 325° for 1 ½ hour.

Remove from cookie sheet while still hot. Cool and slice.

DATE NUT BARS
....
Alba Panasci

1 c. Crisco
⅔ c. milk
1 tsp. vanilla
3 c. flour
1 c. sugar
6 tsp. baking powder
6 eggs
2 Ibs. dates
1 c. chopped nuts

Preheat oven to 350°. Cream Crisco, sugar, eggs, and vanilla. Add dates, dry ingredients, and milk alternately. Bake in a greased 15 x 10½-inch cookie sheet for 30 minutes. Cool. Sprinkle with powdered sugar and cut into squares.

DATE NUT BARS

....

Mary F. Lanzi

1 ¼ c. chopped nuts
3 eggs
1 ½ c. sugar
1 Tbsp, vanilla
1 c. oil
1 lb. chopped dates
1 ½ c. flour
1 ½ tsp. baking powder
1 dash salt
Confectionary sugar

Mix eggs, sugar, vanilla, and oil together. Add dry ingredients, dates, and nuts. Bake in an 11 x 15-inch pan at 350° oven until brown, about 25 to 30 minutes. Top with confectioners sugar.

DATE SHEET COOKIES

....

Mrs. Mary Mosca

2 lb. pitted dates
6 eggs
½ c. spray
½ c. sugar
1 tsp. baking powder
2 ½ c. flour
1 c. chopped nuts

Mix shortening, eggs, and sugar. Add chopped dates and nuts. Add dry ingredients.

Spread on a greased cookie sheet and bake at 350° for 40 minutes.

When cooled, sprinkle with confectionery sugar and cut into squares.

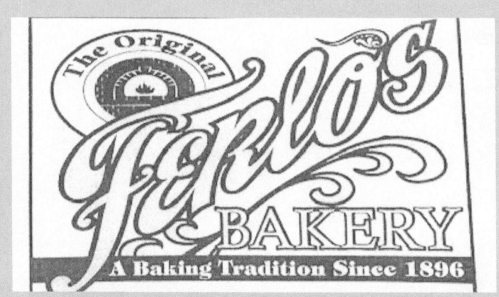
16

DOLLY FLAVER'S CHOCOLATE MINCEMEAT COOKIES

Barbara Amoroso

"This recipe was one of my mother's favorite cookies to bake at Christmas. She would say the mincemeat made the cookies extra moist and tasty and the spices would make the kitchen smell so nice. I miss baking with her. We had so much fun baking together. When I make this special recipe, I feel she is there guiding me."

1 cup Crisco - vegetable shortening
2 1/2 cups sugar
4 eggs
½ cup milk (not skim)
5 tsp baking powder
1 orange: grated rind and juice
½ tsp salt
½ cup cocoa
1 tsp cinnamon

1 tsp cloves
1 tsp ginger
1 cup walnuts – coarsely chopped
1 cup mincemeat
1 pkg semi-sweet chocolate chips
3 tsp vanilla
Flour -- as much as it takes (for a soft
dough use about 6 cups)

I use my stand mixer as it makes a large batch; cream shortening; add sugar gradually, creaming until light; Add eggs and beat thoroughly; Add milk, baking powder, orange rind and juice, salt, and vanilla; Add cinnamon, cloves, ginger, and cocoa continue beating until creamy; Add mincemeat, chocolate chips and chopped nuts, mix until dough is smooth. Add flour 1/2 cup at a time and beat on low speed until you have enough flour to make a soft dough. (Approximately 6 cups).

Line at least 4 large cookie sheets with parchment paper. Shape dough into balls the size of a small walnut and place on prepared cookie sheets. Heat oven to 350 degrees and bake for 12-14 minutes or until set, but not brown. Let stand for a few minutes and then cool on wire racks. Once the cookies are cool, frost them with your favorite frosting. They freeze well.

FUDGE FILLED COOKIES

A Friend

Dough:
4 eggs
¼ c. oil
½ c. sugar

Filling:
1 pkg. chocolate chips
1 can condensed milk
1 ½ tsp. lemon extract
4 tsp. baking powder
About 4 c. flour
1 can walnuts
1 sq. chocolate

Mix dough ingredients together and roll into strips. After melting and thickening the filling ingredients, spoon onto dough strips; fold strips in half and bake at 400° until brown.

Cut into diagonal pieces after cooling.

HALF MOON COOKIES

Rosemary Maio

1 ½ c. sugar
¾ c. shortening
2 eggs
3 c. flour
1 tsp. baking powder
½ tsp. salt
1 tsp. baking soda
1 c. sour milk
1 tsp. vanilla

Cream sugar and shortening; add eggs and beat well. Sift flour, baking powder, and salt. Add soda to sour milk, and slowly add the flour mixture to creamed mixture. Add vanilla. Drop on greased cookie sheets according to the size you want. Bake at 375° for 10 to 12 minutes. Allow cookies to cool and then frost the cookies with half chocolate and half white frosting.

"As a young girl, my mother and I would walk to Rome's downtown and, after our clothes shopping was done, we would stop into the Mohegan Market. They had a fabulous meat counter and also the best baked goods. As my Mom's meat orders were being wrapped, I knew what was coming next: half-dozen of Half Moon Cookies! Yeah! I was given the task to carry the box of Half Moons home. Oh, the excitement!"– MaryAnn Rotolo

HALF MOON COOKIES

Mrs. Angeline Messineo

1 c. sour milk
1 ½ c. sugar
¾ c. shortening
2 eggs
3 c. flour
1 teaspoon baking soda
1 tsp. baking powder
1 tsp. vanilla
½ tsp. salt

Cream sugar and shortening and add eggs. Beat well. Sift together the flour, baking powder, and salt. Add baking soda to the sour milk. Add this alternately with the flour mixture. Add vanilla and bake on cookie sheets at 375°.

These are drop cookies.

When cool, frost half of each cookie with vanilla frosting and the other half with chocolate frosting.

HONEY COOKIES

Luigina Curcio

1 (1 lb. 12 oz.) box Cream of Wheat
1 ½ boxes flour (measure in Cream of Wheat box)
2 Tbsp. cloves, ground
2 Tbsp. cinnamon, ground
1 c. granulated sugar
2 c. Wesson oil
1 c. water
1 c. wine (any kind)
1 c. whiskey
½ c. honey

Mix Cream of Wheat, flour, cloves, cinnamon, and sugar in a large bowl. Make a well in the center of the mixture.

In a saucepan, warm water, wine, and whiskey. Next, pour the sauce mixture into the center of the dry ingredient well. Mix with hands, if the mixture doesn't stay together, add a little more flour (mix with a light hand).

Heat oil in a large cast iron pan. Roll cookie mixture into 1-inch thick - cut into 1 ½ inches pieces - on a grooved board.

Drop cookies into hot oil and fry on one side until brown. Then turn and fry on the other side. Drain the cookies in a colander.

Next, place honey in a saucepan and heat. Then drizzle honey over the cookies and sprinkle with cinnamon and sugar. Cover with aluminum foil and tie down with rubber bands.

"I lived next door to Louis and Rose Curcio, Luigina's brother and sister-in-law. Luigina shared her recipe with Rose. Rose baked these honey cookies frequently, named "Crustas" in Italian. She often shared these delicious cookies with my family. Made with Farina, fried and then rolled in honey, this recipe was originally brought over from Calabria, Italy. Italian Honey Cookies are like bits of fried heaven!" – MaryAnn Rotolo

HONEY SLICES

Jennie Sanzone

1 c. flour
1 tsp. baking powder
½ tsp. cinnamon
½ c. chopped walnuts
½ c. shortening
3 eggs (reserve 1 egg white)
½ c. honey

Warm honey slightly and add all ingredients. Mix until you form a manageable dough.

Roll dough into an oblong loaf about 3 inches wide and ½ inch thick and place on a greased cookie sheet.

Brush the top of the loaf with reserved egg white. Bake at 350° for 30 minutes and cut into 1 inch slices.

HORNS OR KIFEL

Bonnie Farraggio

½ lb. oleo
3 c. flour
3 egg yolks
1 yeast (dry or regular)
1 Tbsp. sugar
½ tsp. vanilla
½ c. milk

Dissolve yeast in warm milk.

Mix flour, sugar, and oleo, as you would a pie crust. Add yeast, egg yolks, and vanilla to the flour mixture. Mix ingredients and then knead on a lightly floured board and shape into a loaf. Divide dough into 6 pieces. Roll each piece to about 6 to 8 inches in diameter.

Sprinkle with cinnamon and sugar and also chopped nuts; optional - you may spread some strawberry preserves on. Then divide this as you would cut a pie.

Roll each piece from the wide end to the narrow. Let them rise for 20 minutes. Bake at 350° until browned.

ITALIAN BISCUITS (BISCOTTI)

Sally Mungari

6 c. flour
6 eggs
½ c. melted Spry
1 ½ c. oil
1 orange rind and juice
1 ½ c. milk
1 ½ c. sugar
6 tsp. baking powder (level)
1 tsp. Salt

Mix sugar, oil, eggs, Spry, orange rind, and juice. Then add milk alternately with dry ingredients. Shape into twists or crescents.

Bake at 375° for 15 minutes.

ITALIAN BISCOTTI

Mrs. Henry Baptiste

4 c. flour
1 tsp. salt
6 tsp baking powder
1 c. sugar
8 Tbsp. shortening
4 eggs
1 c. milk
1 tsp. vanilla

In a large bowl, sift salt, flour, and baking powder. Cut in shortening, eggs, milk, and vanilla. The mixture may be sticky, if so add more flour until it is easy to handle.

Take small pieces of the dough and shape them into circles or crescents or twists. Place on a greased cookie sheet and bake at 400° for 10 to 12 minutes.

ITALIAN COOKIES

Mary Contese

4 eggs
1 c. sugar
1 c. oleo (melt and cool)
1 tsp. vanilla
1 tsp. lemon extract
1 to 5 c. flour
6 heaping tsp. baking powder
1 c. milk

Beat eggs; add sugar and continue beating. Add oleo, milk, and extracts. Then add flour and baking powder.

Place on floured board; knead and shape cookies as desired. Place on greased sheet.

Bake at 375° for 15 minutes.

ITALIAN DATE COOKIES

Bonnie Farraggio

6 c. flour
1 lb. Crisco
1 c. sugar
1 tsp. baking powder
1 tsp. baking soda
1 c. orange juice
4 egg yolks

Add flour, sugar, baking soda, and baking powder to a bowl; cut in Crisco.

Beat egg yolks and add them with orange juice to make a nice soft dough.

Filling:
1 lb. dates, cut up
1 lb. chopped walnuts
½ c. water
¾ c. sugar
1 (12 oz.) jar grape jam

Cook dates, water, and sugar until thick. Then add jam and nuts.

Roll out like pie crust; fill with filling; roll into loaves. Brush top with beaten egg yolk. Bake at 375° for 15 to 20 minutes.

ITALIAN PIZZELLE

Mary F. Lanzi

6 eggs, beaten
1 c. sugar
⅔ c. oil
1 tsp. lemon flavor
Flour - enough to make a
batter that will ripple
when poured

Add and beat ingredients together in the order listed.

Drop a rounded spoonful onto the center of a preheated pizzelle iron. Close the lid and allow to cook until steaming stops - about 30 seconds or until the desired brownness you prefer.

Remove with a fork and cool on a wire rack.

**Pizzelle stay fresh and crisp if you do not store them in an airtight container. Just cover them loosely with a paper towel.

"Very few people remember the old way we made pizzelle. Today, with the electric machines, you can sit and make them. As a kid, we stood over the gas stove and flipped the pizzelle iron one at a time. Thank God for technology!" – Patti Martinelli

ITALIAN PIZZELLI

Mrs. Christine Vito

3 ½ dozen eggs
1 lb. Crisco
1 qt. oil
10 c. granulated sugar
14 ½ lb. all-purpose flour
2 Tbsp. salt
2 Tbsp. baking powder
1 small box anise seeds
2 lemon juice
2 orange juice
¾ bottle pure vanilla extract

Place pizzelle cast iron on a gas flame, then place the small batch of dough (the size of a walnut) on it.

*Makes about one bushel.

LEMON COCONUT COOKIES

Mrs. Dom. Favata

1 c. shortening, melted and cooled
1 c. sugar
6 tsp. lemon extract
1 lb. pound coconut, chopped fine
6 eggs
6 heaping tsp. baking powder
4 or 5 c. flour

Mix shortening and sugar. Add eggs, baking powder, and lemon extract. Add enough flour to form a soft dough and add coconut. Shape in small balls and place about two inches apart on a baking sheet.

Bake at 375° for 10 to 12 minutes.

Frost with butter frosting, use lemon flavoring.

MA'S WINE COOKIES

Delcie Castro

1 ¾ c. oil
1 pt. (2 c.) white wine
2 c. sugar
¼ c. anise seed
1 ½ lb. flour
2 tsp. baking powder
1 egg white

Using a Mix-master, mix in oil, wine, sugar, and seeds.

Add flour and baking powder to the mixture and mix them together. The dough will be very sticky. If too sticky, add a little more flour until the dough is manageable.

Shape cookies in an S shape or donut form and brush each cookie with beaten egg white and sprinkle with sugar.

Bake at 350° for 15 minutes.

"I have found memories of Delcie and Patty who are identical twin sisters. Patty is a cousin to me through marriage to Joseph "Joe" Froio, my first cousin. Both Delcie and Patty were amazing cooks and bakers. I have made these wine cookies many times. I promise you won't be disappointed!"– MaryAnn Rotolo

MINCEMENT COOKIES

Mrs. Romeo Bucknell, Sr.

¾ c. margarine or butter
1 cup brown sugar
1 egg beaten
1 tsp. vanilla
2 ½ c. sifted flour
½ tsp. salt
½ tsp. baking soda
1 tsp. cinnamon
½ c. minced meat
1 c. chopped nuts

Cream the sugar and shortening. Add egg.

Sift all dry ingredients and add to sugar mixture. Blend thoroughly. Drop by spoonfuls on greased cookie sheet. Bake at 350° for 15 minutes.

*Makes four dozen.

MOLASSES COOKIES

Mrs. Pauline Gratch

½ c. shortening
½ c. sugar
½ c. molasses
1 egg
½ c. water

Sift together, then add:

2 tsp baking soda
1 tsp cinnamon
¼ tsp nutmeg
¼ tsp ginger
¼ tsp cloves
2 ¾ cups cup flour

Bake at 360° for 15 minutes.

MOLASSES COOKIES

Rose Rossi

1 c. shortening
1 c. molasses
1 c. sugar
1 egg
1 c. water
5 c. flour
2 tsp. baking soda
2 tsp. cinnamon
1 tsp. cloves
2 tsp. nutmeg
1 tsp. salt

Cream shortening and sugar (push to one side of the bowl); beat eggs on another side. Blend mixture in bowl.

Mix molasses with water; sift together all dry ingredients and add alternately with liquid, beating enough to mix.

Drop by teaspoonfuls on greased cookie sheet.

Bake at 375° for 15 minutes.

MOMMA JU'S CHOCOLATE CHIP COOKIES

Mary Fahey

"This chocolate chip cookie recipe was one my mom came up with. After my dad passed away she would keep herself busy by baking at night. Since she lived across the street from my family she would start baking at around 9pm at night. All of a sudden at around 9:30-10 she would call and tell me to send either my husband Gary or our daughter Kaitlin over to get some hot cookies that she had just taken out of the oven. One or the other "ran" over to her house! When they came back the cookies were gobbled up in seconds and the smell was heavenly!"

1 cup salted butter-room temperature
1 cup shortening
2 cups packed brown sugar
1 cup granulated sugar
4 eggs room temperature
5 ½- 6 cups flour
2 ½ tsp. baking soda
2 T. vanilla
(I put in a little more cause I like vanilla)
2 12oz. bags semisweet chocolate chips

Beat first 4 ingredients until smooth. Add eggs and vanilla. Combine flour and baking soda and then add to the batter. Once all is combined add the chocolate chips. Bake 375° for 10-13 min.

*Note-I like mine gooey so I cook mine for 9-10 min. and let them set for a few minutes. I also cook mine on parchment paper.

MOLASSES COOKIES

Margo Taylor

"This is my Dad's favorite cookie. Mom got this recipe from her mother, and she used to make it all the time. She then passed the recipe down to her five girls. You have to get the dough chilled just right, and the oven needs to be the exact temp in order to get the cookie to crinkle properly."

¾ c butter, melted
1 c. granulated sugar
¼ c. molasses
1 egg
2 c. all purpose flour
2 tsp. baking soda
½ tsp. cloves
½ tsp. ginger
1 tsp. cinnamon
½ tsp. salt

Add sugar to melted butter and mix well with a mixer. Add molasses and egg. Mix well. Sift dry ingredients. Add to wet ingredients. Mix well. Chill in the refrigerator for at least an hour. Roll into 1" balls and roll in sugar before placing on an ungreased cookie sheet. Bake in a pre-heated 350 degree oven for 12 minutes. Cool on the pan for a few minutes before moving it to a cooling rack. Enjoy!

NEOPOLITAN COOKIES

Shirley Nasci

Basic Dough:
2 ½ c. all-purpose flour
1 ½ c. sugar
1 c. butter or margarine, softened
1 ½ tsp. double acting baking powder
1 tsp. vanilla extract

½ tsp. salt
½ tsp. almond extract
½ c. chopped walnuts
Red food color

In a large bowl, mix all ingredients at low speed. Beat until fully mixed and then increase speed and beat for an additional three minutes.

Line a 9 x 5-inch loaf pan with waxed paper. Spoon ⅓ basic dough mixture into a small bowl; stir in almond extract and 5 drops of red food coloring until well mixed. Spread evenly into a waxed paper-lined pan.

Spoon half of the remaining dough into another small bowl; stir in chopped walnuts until well mixed. Spread evenly over almond-flavored dough.

Stir in 1 square of unsweetened melted chocolate into the remaining dough. Spread evenly over walnut dough. Cover loaf pan and refrigerate until firm, about 4 hours.

Preheat oven to 350°. Remove dough from pan and peel off waxed paper. Cut dough lengthwise in half. Slice each half crosswise into ½ inch slices and place on an ungreased sheet. Bake 10 to 12 minutes until light brown.

Remove to cool.

NUT ROLLS

....

Josephine R. Calandra

5 Tbsp. sugar (granulated)
2 Tbsp. brown sugar
2 sticks oleo
2 c. flour
1 tsp. vanilla
⅓ tsp. salt
2 c. pecans and walnuts, crushed
Confectioners sugar

Mix all ingredients together. Roll into balls and bake at 300° for 20 minutes. Then turn the oven down to 250° and bake for an additional 15 minutes.

While still hot, shake in a bag with confectioners sugar.

PEANUT CLUSTERS

....

Mrs. Bambina Schillaci

½ lb of chocolate
⅔ cup (1/2 can) condensed milk
1 c. whole peanuts or raisins

Melt chocolate in top of a double boiler over boiling water. Remove from heat. Add condensed milk and peanuts, mixing well. Drop by teaspoonfuls on buttered baking sheets or plates.

Chill for several hours.

Makes about 26 clusters.

PINEAPPLE COOKIES

....

Mrs. Virginia Pisano

Cream well:

1 c. granulated sugar
⅔ c. shortening

Add 1 egg and beat well. add another egg and repeat.

Then add:

1 small can of crushed pineapple
1 tsp. lemon or vanilla flavoring

Sift 2 cups flour and add to it:

¼ tsp. salt
¼ tsp. baking soda
½ tsp. baking powder

Fold into the cookie mixture. Drop on a cookie sheet and bake for 10 minutes at 400°. Coconut, nutmeats, dates, or raisins may be added if desired.

PINEAPPLE SHEET
. . . .
Marie George

Dough:
2 ½ c. flour
¾ c. sugar
¾ c. Spry
2 ½ tsp. baking powder
½ tsp. baking soda
1 tsp. vanilla
¼ c. milk
2 eggs, slightly beaten

Using a pastry blender, blend flour, sugar, and Spry; add baking powder, baking soda, vanilla, milk, and eggs. Mix and blend well until it forms a ball.

Separate into 2 parts. Set aside.

Filling:

1 large can of crushed pineapple
½ c. sugar
3 Tbsp. flour
1 tsp. Vanilla

Cook the above ingredients over low heat until slightly thickened. Cool. Set aside.

Cut 2 pieces of waxed paper the size of a cookie sheet. Place 1 part of the dough between 2 sheets of waxed paper and roll out as for pie crust (1/4 to 1/2 inch thick). Peel off the top of the waxed paper and turn over the dough onto a cookie sheet.

Peel off the second sheet of waxed paper. Pour and spread pineapple filling on the dough. Roll the second part of the dough as above. Turn over on filling and peel off the waxed paper as above.

Bake at 350° for 25 minutes. DO NOT GREASE TIN.

PINEAPPLE SQUARES
. . . .
Virginia Pisano

3 c. flour
3 tsp. baking powder
½ c. sugar
Pineapple pie filling (canned)
1 tsp. vanilla
3 eggs
½ c. milk
½ c. oil

Sift flour, baking powder, and sugar together. Make a well and add eggs, vanilla, milk, and oil. Mix well.

Roll out half of the dough on a greased and floured cookie sheet. Top with the pineapple pie mix.

Roll the other half of the dough on floured waxed paper and then place it on top of the filling mixture. Spread milk over top of the dough and sprinkle with granulated sugar.

Bake at 375° for 20 to 25 minutes.

PINEAPPLE NUT COOKIES

....

Mrs. Romeo Bucknell, Senior

1 c. shortening
1 c. brown sugar
1 c. crushed pineapple
2 eggs
½ tsp. baking soda
1 tsp. salt
2 tsp baking powder
4 c. flour
2 tsp. vanilla
1 c. chopped nuts

Cream the sugar and shortening. Add eggs and beat well. Add pineapple and flavoring.

Sift flour, baking soda, salt, and baking powder. Add to mixture and add nuts. Drop teaspoon size dough onto a greased cookie sheet. Bake at 400° for 10 minutes.

PINEAPPLE SQUARES

....

Mary F. Lanzi

Dough:
1 c. Crisco
4 c. flour
Dash of salt
2 eggs, slightly beaten
2 tsp. baking soda
1 c. sugar
1 c. sour cream
1 tsp. vanilla
maraschino cherries
Crushed nuts

Beat together shortening, sugar and eggs. Add sour cream, vanilla, baking soda, salt, and flour. CHILL DOUGH.

Filling:
1 c. sugar
3 Tbsp, cornstarch
1 large can of crushed pineapple

Mix all ingredients together and cook on the stovetop for about 5 minutes and cool.

Roll ¾ of the dough on a floured board and place on an ungreased cookie sheet with edges.

Pour filling on top of the dough and spread. Create a fancy lattice work on top of the filling with the remaining dough.

Decorate with maraschino cherries all over the top and sprinkle with crushed nuts. Bake at 350° until brown. Cool and slice into squares.

PLAIN ITALIAN COOKIES

Angeline Gualtieri

1 c. sugar
4 eggs
1 c. melted shortening
1 ½ tsp. vanilla
1 ½ tsp. lemon extract
4 heaping tsp. baking powder
1 c. cold milk
4 c. flour (more if needed)

Cream together sugar, shortening, and eggs. Add vanilla, lemon extract, dry ingredients, and milk.

Roll cookies in donut form or round balls.

Bake at 375° for 15 minutes or more.

Ice with lemon and vanilla icing.

RICOTTA COOKIES

Julia Strange

1 c. margarine
1 tsp. vanilla
1 tsp. lemon flavoring
3½ c. sifted flour
1 c. ricotta
2 c. sugar
2 eggs
2 tsp. baking soda
1 tsp. salt

Mix together. Bake at 350° for 12 minutes until lightly brown.

SOUR CREAM COOKIES

Marie Minnie Wightman

2 eggs
1 pl. sour cream
½ c. Spry
1 tsp. baking powder
1 ½ c. sugar
1 tsp. baking soda
3 c. flour
1 tsp. nutmeg

Beat eggs and add in Spry and sugar. Stir in sour cream, baking powder, baking soda, and nutmeg.

Stir in 3 cups of flour until blended.

Drop a tablespoon size of dough on a greased and floured cookie sheet. Sprinkle sugar on top.

Bake at 350°.

TEA TIME TASSIES

Jennie Stromick

Dough:
1 (3 oz.) pkg. cream cheese
½ c. butter

Filling:
1 c. coarsely chopped pecans
¾ c. brown sugar
1 Tbsp. vanilla
1 c. flour
1 Tbsp. sugar
1 dash salt
1 egg

Use miniature cupcake tins.

Roll out the dough and fit it into muffin tins. Drop the filling into the lined tins.

Bake at 375° for about 25 minutes.

WANDS (ITALIAN BOWS)

Sue Rossi

6 eggs
3 Tbsp. lemon
1 c. sugar (heaping)
Lemon rind (optional)
1 Tbsp, shortening
3 c. flour, sifted

Beat eggs; add sugar, lemon rind, and shortening. Mix in flour and knead the dough.

Let stand for ½ hour covered.

Knead the dough and make it into wand shapes by rolling the dough and cutting strips, then tying in a knot.

Fry in deep oil.

Sprinkle with powdered sugar.

WARTIME MOLASSES COOKIES

Mrs. Joseph Squallace

3 Tbsp. lard
2 Tbsp. boiling water
1 tsp. baking soda
Pinch of salt
1 tsp. ginger
1 c. molasses
1 c. flour or enough to mix like cake

Mix all ingredients together; and spread on a cookie sheet.

Bake at 350° for 12 minutes or more.

When done cut into squares.

WINE COOKIES

Mrs. Inessa Darkangelo

2 c. sugar
8 c. flour
5 tsp. baking powder
3 c. white wine
1 c. Mazola oil
½ tsp. nutmeg
1 grated lemon rind and juice

Mix dry ingredients. Add wine, oil, lemon rind and juice, and mix well.

Roll dough onto a half-inch thickness. Cut the dough 3 inches in length and shape and different designs.

Dip each cookie in sugar and place right side up on grease cookie sheet. Bake at 450° for 25 minutes.

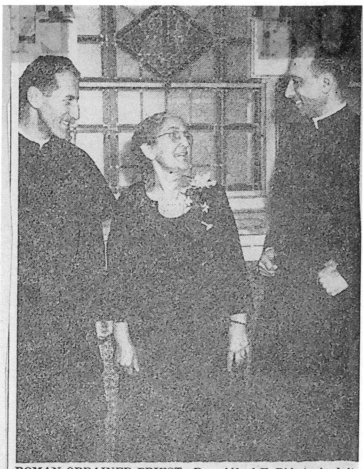

ROMAN ORDAINED PRIEST—Rev. Alfred F. D'Antonio, left, ordained to Roman Catholic priesthood Saturday in Washington, D. C., celebrated his first solemn Mass yesterday at St. John the Baptist Church. Pictured with Father D'Antonio, prior to afternoon reception, are his mother, Mrs. Alfonsina D'Antonio, 136 River St., and Rev. Victor F. Ciciarelli, pastor of St. John's.

GRANOLA

CRUNCHY GRANOLA

Ann Grasso

4 c. old-fashioned oats
1 (4 oz.) can of shredded coconut
½ c. sesame seed
½ c. sunflower seed
½ c. toasted or untoasted wheat germ
¾ tsp. cinnamon
½ tsp. nutmeg
½ c. honey
½ c. oil
1 c. raisins

In a large bowl combine oats, coconut, sesame seed, sunflower seed, wheat germ, cinnamon, and nutmeg. Add honey and oil; mix well.

Pour onto 2 cookie sheets, and spread thin. Bake at 275° for 30 minutes.

Cool and crumble. Add raisins. Store in a tightly covered container and refrigerate.

Yield: 10 cups.

GRANOLA

Lucille Barnett

2 ½ c. whole wheat flour
½ c. millet flour
½ c. almond or pecan meal
½ c. sesame seed
2 ½ c. rolled oats
1 c. cornmeal
½ c. rye flour
1 c. shredded coconut
¾ c. water
½ c. dates
1 c. brown sugar or honey
3/3 c. oil
½ c. nuts
1 tsp. vanilla
2 tsp. salt

In a blender mix water, dates, brown sugar or honey, oil, nuts, vanilla, and salt. Blend in dry ingredients and mix until crumbly.

Place granola in a large flat pan such as cookie sheets and bake at 275° for 1 ½ hour, or until golden brown. Stir frequently.

Yield: 2 quarts.

PIES & CRISPS

APPLE CRISP

Sue Rossi

3 c. sliced apples or peaches
2 Tbsp. water
¼ to ⅓ c. sugar
1 ¼ c. Bisquick
½ c. sugar
½ tsp. cinnamon
1 egg
¼ c. margarine, melted

Heat oven to 400°.
Place fruit in a greased oblong or square pan. Sprinkle water and sugar over the fruit. Mix Bisquick, sugar, and cinnamon. Beat egg thoroughly. Pour slowly over the Bisquick mixture in a thin stream, constantly stirring with a fork until crumbly. Sprinkle mixture over fruit. Pour butter over all.
Bake for about 25 minutes or until brown.

Serve hot or cold with milk or cream.

6 to 8 servings.

BLUEBERRY PIE

Ange Tallarino

1 c. blueberries
3/4 c. water
1 c. sugar

Boil until soft, 3 to 5 minutes. Add 2 tablespoons cornstarch (mixed with a little cold water). Stir over heat until mixture is thick. Add 3 cups raw blueberries.

Pour into baked pie shell. Cool. Top with whipped cream.

BROWN SUGAR RHUBARB PIE

Kay DelPiano

Pastry for single-crust pie
Bake pastry in a 450° oven for 5 minutes. Cool.

Filling:
1 to 1¼ c. packed brown sugar
¼ c. all-purpose flour
¼ tsp. salt
4 c. (1 Ib.) diced rhubarb
3 eggs
1 T. lemon juice
Meringue for pie

To prepare filling:

Combine brown sugar, flour, and salt. Add brown sugar mixture to rhubarb. Toss to coat fruit. Let stand for 15 minutes. Separate egg yolks from whites; set whites aside for meringue. Beat yolks slightly with a fork. Stir yolks and lemon juice into the rhubarb mixture.

Turn rhubarb filling into a partially baked pastry shell. Reduce oven temperature to 375°; cover edge with foil and bake for 25 minutes. Remove foil; bake for 20-25 minutes more or until nearly set. (Pie appears soft in the center but becomes firm after cooling.) Spread meringue over hot filling; seal to edge. Reduce oven temperature to 350° and bake for 12 to 15 minutes. Cool and chill.

CHOCOLATE FUDGE PIE

Mrs. Joanne Lloyd

1 ¾ squares baker's chocolate
¼ lb. butter or margarine
2 eggs
1 c. sugar
¼ c. flour
1 tsp vanilla

Melt chocolate and butter together. Beat in eggs, sugar, flour, and vanilla.

Place ingredients in a buttered pie pan and bake at 350° for 25 minutes.

Top with ice cream or whipped cream.

CHOCOLATE FUNNY CAKE PIE

Crystal D'Ambrosi

"My mom used to make this pie along with a shoo fly pie every year around the holidays. My favorite was always the chocolate funny cake pie. My sister-in-law Debbie has continued this tradition. She makes the chocolate funny cake pie every Thanksgiving, and she always includes extra pies to take home with us. It's so good!"

1 unbaked pie shell
1 Cup sugar
1/4 Cup shortening
1/2 Cup milk
1 egg
1 Cup flour
1 teaspoon baking powder
1/2 teaspoon vanilla

Mix all ingredients together and pour into an unbaked pie shell. In a clean bowl, mix together:

½ Cup sugar
¼ Cup cocoa
6 Tablespoons boiling water
¼ teaspoon vanilla

Pour the chocolate sauce over the cake mixture and bake at 350 degrees for 45-55 minutes. A toothpick inserted into the center should come out clean when it's done—if not, give it a little more time.

"Whenever I see a pie, I think of my father. He would like to have pie for breakfast!"
- Father Joseph Sestito

COCONUT CREAM PIE

Barbara Amoroso

Crust:
1 c. flour
1 stick butter or margarine, melted
½ c. chopped nuts

Mix flour and nuts together, then pour melted butter into the flour mixture and pat in a 9-or 10-inch pie plate.

Bake at 350° for 10 minutes. Cool.

Filling:
4 T. cornstarch
4 c. milk
Dash salt
1 c. sugar
1 tsp. vanilla
4 egg yolks
Chunk of butter
1½ to 2 c. coconut

Mix the above ingredients together (except butter, vanilla, and coconut) in a saucepan. Cook until thickened. When thick, stir in the chunk of butter, vanilla, and coconut. Pour pudding into baked crust and refrigerate until cold.

You can top it with heavy cream or meringue.

GRAHAM CRACKER PIE

Deborah Ceresoli

3 egg whites
1 c. granulated sugar
12 single graham crackers, rolled into crumbs
1 rounded tsp. baking powder
1/2 c. chopped nutmeats

Beat whites until stiff; fold in granulated sugar; add nutmeats.

Grease a 9-inch pie tin and spread evenly with graham crackers and baking powder.

Pour the egg white mixture into the pie shell and spread evenly.

Bake at 350° for 1/2 hour.

Serve topped with whipped cream or ice cream.

HEAVENLY PIE

....

Mrs. Lewell E. Isom

1 ½ c. granulated sugar
¼ tsp cream of tartar
4 egg whites
4 egg yolks
3 Tbsp. lemon juice
1 Tbsp. grated lemon rind
⅛ tsp. salt
1 c. evaporated milk, chilled
graham cracker crumbs.

Heat oven to 275°. Sift 1 c. of sugar with the cream of tartar.

Separate eggs and beat egg whites until they stand stiff. Slowly add sugar to the egg whites, while beating until stiff glossy peaks appear. Spread the egg whites over the bottom upsides and the rim of a well-greased 9-inch pie plate, making the bottom ¼ inch thick and the sides one inch thick.

Bake at 275° for one hour, until the top is lightly brown and crisp. Let it cool.

In the meantime, beat egg yolks on top of a double boiler. Stir in sugar, lemon juice, grated lemon rind, and salt. Remove from the stove.

When the mixture cools add evaporated milk and fold it into the custard. By this time the meringue shells should be cool enough to fill. Slowly pour the cooled mixture into the center of the meringue, making sure all the little pockets are filled and smooth.

Put the pie in the refrigerator and chill for at least 12 hours.

Just before serving, sprinkle with graham crackers.

*Good to make a day ahead.

ITALIAN CHERRY CHEESE PIE

....

Mary Cortese

1 c. flour
1/4 c. sugar
1 tsp. baking powder
1/2 tsp. salt
6 Tbsp. butter
1 egg
1 (4 oz.) jar maraschino cherries
1 (8 oz.) pkg. softened cream cheese
1/3 c. sugar
1 c. Ricotta cheese
2 eggs, separated
3 Tbsp. flour
1/2 tsp. grated lemon rind
1/2 tsp. vanilla
3/4 c. milk

In a medium mixing bowl, stir together flour, 1/4 cup sugar, baking powder and salt; cut in shortening until crumbly. Add whole egg and stir until well-mixed. Press dough over bottom and sides of a 9 inch pie plate, fluted edge. Drain cherries, cut in halves and drain. In another bowl, beat cream cheese and 1/3 cup sugar, blend in Ricotta cheese, 2 egg yolks, 3 tablespoons flour, lemon rind and vanilla. Stir in milk. Beat 2 egg whites until stiff; fold into cheese mixture. Place cherries in pie shell and add cheese filling. Bake at 300° until knife inserted in center comes out clean. Bake 1 hour.

IMPOSSIBLE PIE
....
Jenny Guggi

1 egg
1 1/4 c. margarine
1 c. milk
1/2 c. sugar
1/2 c. coconut
1/2 c. biscuit mix
1 tsp. vanilla

Blend all ingredients together for two minutes until smooth.
Pour in a buttered 9-inch floured plate and bake at 350° for 45 minutes.
Chill for three hours before serving.

LEMON COCONUT COBBLE
....
Betty Clancy

2 pkg. lemon pudding mix
1 pkg. unflavored gelatin
1 c. sugar
4 egg yolks
1 Angel Food cake
4 c. water
1/4 c. lemon juice
2 Tbsp. grated lemon rind
1 c. heavy cream, whipped
1 (3 1/4 oz.) can of coconut

Mix pudding, gelatin, sugar, egg yolks, and water together and cook over medium heat. When it comes to a boil, remove. Add lemon juice and rind. Let cool.

Fold in heavy cream, whipped, and a can of coconut. Add 1 Angel Food cake, cut up into small cubes.

Butter a pan and fill with filling. Refrigerate overnight. Serve with Cool Whip or whipped cream or plain.

LEMON SPONGE PIE
....
Mrs. Angela Ghisalbert

Cream together:
1 c. white sugar
1 Tbsp butter
2 level Tbsp. flour
pinch salt
juice and grated rind of one lemon
2 egg yolks, well-beaten
1 c. of milk
2 egg whites

Cream ingredients together and fold in an unbaked pie crust.

Bake at 275°.

PISTACHIO PIE
. . . .
Mary F. Lanzi

1 lb. fine Ricotta cheese
1 Tbsp. sugar
1 1/2 c. milk
1 pkg. pistachio instant pudding
1 9-inch graham cracker, vanilla
wafer, or zwieback pie crust
Cool Whip
Maraschino cherries

Filling: Beat Ricotta cheese and sugar; add 1/2 cup milk and continue beating until smooth. Add remaining milk and pudding.

Pour into the pie shell of choice and garnish with Cool Whip. Top with cherries if desired.

PIZZA DOLCE
. . . .
Evelyn Catania

Crust:
4 c. flour
¼ c. water
1 c. sugar
4 to 6 egg yolks
1 c. shortening

Mix the flour and sugar; cut in shortening and make a well and add the water and egg yolks.

Roll crust out to fit a deep 10-inch pan or make 2 small pies (preferably a deep pie plate). Save half the crust for a lattice top.

Cream Filling for Pizza Dolce:

Mix together in a saucepan the following:
1 qt. milk
Lemon rind, sliced
1 ½ c. sugar
Few sticks cinnamon
1 c. flour
8 egg yolks

In a saucepan, cook the above ingredients over medium heat until thick, stirring constantly. Pour into an unbaked pie shell and bake at 350° until lightly browned.

RICE PIE
....
Clotilde Cavallaro

Crust:
4 c. flour
½ lb. shortening
1 tsp. salt
1 egg
1 tsp. baking powder
About 1 c. water

Mix all together. Form into dough and roll out.

Filling:

1 lb. ricotta
3 c. cooked rice
6 or 7 eggs
3 c. milk
2 c. sugar
Cinnamon & vanilla to taste

Mix all above ingredients together. Put in unbaked pie shell. Put strips across the top. Brush on egg yolk. Bake at 350° for 1 hour. When done, sprinkle top with cinnamon and sugar.

RICE AND RICOTTA PIES
....
By: Felicia Combopiano

Filling:
1 lb. raw rice
1 qt. of half milk and water or skim milk
1 lb. Ricotta cheese
18 eggs
2 c. sugar
1 Tbsp. butter
1 tsp. vanilla
1/2 tsp. nutmeg
1 tsp. cinnamon

Rind and juice of lemon and orange
1 bar semi-sweet chocolate, cut up into small pieces

Crust (double crust for 4 pies):

2 c. flour
4 Tbsp. sugar
4 Tbsp. oleo or butter
2 tsp. baking powder
1/2 c. milk
1 tsp. vanilla
3 eggs

Blend together to make the crust; this makes 2 (10-inch) pies. Make a lattice top. Bon Appetit.

RICOTTA PIE

Mary F. Lanzi

"I've used Mary Lanzi's Ricotta Pie recipe since the '70's and I can honestly say this this by far the best recipe you will find." – MaryAnn Rotolo

1/4 lb. butter
1 orange (rind and juice)
1 Hershey chocolate bar
1 lb. fine Ricotta cheese
1/2 c. sugar
1 jigger whiskey
Glazed fruit if desired
8 eggs, beaten
1/2 tsp. lemon juice
Dash cinnamon

In a saucepan, melt 1/4 pound of butter together with 1 orange rind (you may also melt the chocolate bar with the butter if desired). Optional - you may sliver the chocolate bar and add it to the filling when it is all mixed.

Beat Ricotta cheese; slowly add sugar, whiskey, glazed fruit (if desired), 8 beaten eggs, juice of orange, 1/2 teaspoon lemon juice, and a dash of cinnamon.

Fold in butter mixture.

Pour into crust, make a lattice top and bake at 300° for 1 1/2 hours.

RICOTTA RICE PIE

Mary F. Lanzi

1/2 to 3/4 c. rice
2 1/2 c. boiling water
2 c. milk
1 Tbsp. butter
1 c. sugar
1 lb. Ricotta cheese
9 eggs
1 tsp. cinnamon
1/2 c. citron or orange peel,
if desired

Cook rice in 2 1/2 cups of boiling water until done. Drain and rinse with hot water. Set aside.

In a separate pan, add 2 cups milk, 1 tablespoon butter, and 2 cups sugar; cook until soft. Note: this will not get thick.
Meanwhile, beat Ricotta cheese until smooth; add eggs, one at a time, cinnamon, and citron or orange peel. Pour in the milk mixture, and add the rice mixture.

Pour into pie shell.

Bake for 1 hour at 350°.

CRUST FOR RICOTTA AND RICE PIES

Shirley Lanzi

6 c. flour
1 1/2 c. shortening
(Spry or Crisco)
6 eggs
4 tsp. lemon flavoring
2 c. sugar
1/2 c. milk
6 tsp. baking powder

With a mixer, cream shortening, sugar, and eggs. Add lemon flavoring, milk, baking powder, and flour. The dough will be hard to handle. Do not add more than 6 cups of flour.

Roll crust out between 2 sheets of waxed paper. If this crust should break when you are putting it in your pan, do not hesitate to just patch it together.

SOUTHERN PECAN PIE

Mrs. Dominick Marchione

3 eggs
1/3 c. sugar
1 c. dark corn syrup
1/3 c. melted butter or oleo
1 c. pecan halves
1 (9 inch) unbaked pastry shell

Beat eggs thoroughly with sugar, dash of salt, corn syrup and melted butter. Add pecans. Pour into unbaked pastry shell. Bake in moderate oven (350°) for 50 minutes or until knife inserted halfway between outside and center of filling comes out clean. Let cool before serving.

PASTRIES

• •

APPLE STRUDEL
. . . .
Mrs. Angeline Amoroso

1 ½ c. flour
¾ c. sugar
3 tsp baking powder
½ tsp salt
½ c. apples
1 tsp cinnamon
¼ c. brown sugar
¼ c. Spry shortening
1 egg
½ c. milk
1 tsp vanilla
1 tsp butter
nuts

Sift dry ingredients and cut in Spry. Add milk, egg, and vanilla.

Spread half the batter on the bottom of the pan. Cut apples and place them on top. Then spread the rest of the batter on top. Add brown sugar, butter, and nuts.

Bake at 375° for 25 to 30 minutes.

CREAM PUFFS
. . . .
Mrs. Beatrice Cangi

4 eggs
½ c. oil
1 c. water
1 c. flour

Boil water and oil together. Take off of the stove and add in flour. Beat until smooth.

Place the mixture back on the stove and heat until the dough is all together. Then, take off the stove, and add eggs - one at a time. Continue mixing until all eggs are in.

On an ungreased cookie sheet drop a Tbsp. of the mixture.

Bake at 450° for 25 minutes. Then turn over and lower the oven to 325° and bake for an additional 20 minutes.

Filling for cream puffs:
¾ c. sugar
2 egg yolks
4 Tbsp cornstarch
vanilla
¾ qt. milk

Mix the top four ingredients. Then add milk and boil on a double broiler; cook until thick. Then add the remaining ingredients.

*Make sure to stir constantly for a smooth cream.

CREAM PUFF SHELLS

Miss Catherine Diodato

½ c. shortening
1 c. water
1 c. flour
4 eggs

Bring shortening and water to boiling point.; add flour. Stir until you have a smooth paste.

Remove from heat; add eggs, one at a time, beating thoroughly after each egg.

Drop by spoonfuls on a greased cookie sheet.

Bake at 375° for approximately 40 minutes. When cool, fill with whipped cream, custard, or pudding.

CREAM PUFF FILLING

Mary F. Lanzi

2 c. milk
3 Tbsp. flour
Dash salt
1 tsp. vanilla
½ c. sugar
1 Tbsp. cornstarch
2 egg yolks
1 tsp. Butter

Scald milk in a double boiler. To this add the flour, salt, sugar, and cornstarch and mix together. When this mixture is thickened, add the beaten egg yolks. Cook until thick.

Remove from heat and add vanilla and butter. Stir several times while cooling.

Msgr. Cicciarelli baptizes Annmarie Rotolo with parents
MaryAnn and Anthony Rotolo (1982)

DANISH PUFF

Donna Capponi Angotti

"Our family loved this memorable recipe. A pinch of love from mom always makes food taste better."

1 c. flour
2 Tbsp. cold water
1/2 cup oleo

Make a pie crust and divide into 2 parts. On ungreased cookie sheet, press With the heel of the hand, make two strips about 3" wide and the length of the cookie sheet.

Bring to boil:
1 cup of water
1/2 cup oleo.

Remove from heat. Add: 1 cup flour and stir until smooth
3 eggs (Add eggs one at a time and stir after each egg)

Add:
¼ tsp salt
1 tsp almond flavor
1 tsp vanilla

Spread half mixture on each pie crust. Bake at 350° for 20 minutes or until golden brown and puffed.

DULCE RAVIOLI (SWEET PASTRIES)

Mrs. Rosario DeMare

1 ¾ c. flour
3 Tbsp. shortening
water
½ c. ricotta
2 Tbsp. granulated sugar
½ tsp. vanilla
powdered sugar
1 whole egg
1 egg yolk

Mix flour and shortening together with just enough very cold water to form a stiff dough. Sprinkle with powdered sugar and roll out on a lightly floured.

Combine the remaining ingredients and use as a filling for the pastry.

Cut dough into three-inch squares. Place one teaspoon of filling on the square of pastry and cover it with another square. Seal the edges securely by pressing them together with the tips of the fork dipped in flour. Then fry in deep top until golden brown.

Cool on paper to absorb oil.

DANISH ALMOND PASTRY

Angie Sbaraglia

1 c. flour
½ c. oleo
2 Tbsp. water
1 c. water
1 tsp. almond extract
1 cup flour
3 eggs

Cut in oleo and sprinkle water. Mix with a fork. Make it into a ball and divide into 2. Pat dough in 2 strips (3 x 12 inches). Place strips 3 inches apart on greased sheet. Bring water and 1/2 cup oleo to a boil; add almond extract.

Remove from heat and stir in flour. When smooth, add 3 eggs, one at a time, beating until smooth. Divide the mixture in half and spread each half over each piece of pastry. Bake at 350° for 60 minutes. Cool.

Frosting:
1 c. confectioners sugar
1 Tbsp. butter
1 Tbsp. milk
½ tsp. almond extract

Cream butter with sugar; add milk and extract. Beat until smooth. Top with frosting and add chopped nuts.

GRISPELLI OR ZEPPOLI

Barbara Biamonte

8 c. flour
1 pkg. dry yeast
1 c. warm water
4 tsp. salt
2 Tbsp. sugar

Dissolve yeast in ½ cup lukewarm water. Add sugar to dissolved yeast.

Make a well in flour; pour in yeast liquid plus 1 ½ cups lukewarm water to make a very soft dough. Add more water if necessary.

Let rise until double. Punch down and let rise again.

Drop at least 1 tablespoon of dough in hot oil. Fry until brown.

Variations: Add raisins or anchovies to the dough before frying.

ITALIAN CANNOLI (SHELLS)

Pauline Smith

3/4 lb. flour (3 c. or little more)
4 oz. shortening
(3/4 stick margarine)
3 good Tbsp. sugar
6 egg yolks
6 Tbsp. milk
Juice and rind of 1 lemon

Squeeze one lemon and the rind of 1 lemon. Mix together and then roll out on
board. Cut in squares. Fry in deep shortening.

Filling:
1 lb. Ricotta cheese
1 box powdered sugar (extra fine
2 Hershey bars with almonds (cut in small pieces, granulated)

Mix together. You may use an electric beater, if desired. Fill shells.

ITALIAN PASTACIOTTI

Eleanor Ferlo

Dough:
2 c. flour
2 c. light brown sugar
¼ tsp. baking powder
¾ c. Crisco
1 egg, slightly beaten
1 tsp. vanilla

Mix ingredients and knead until the dough is not sticky. Roll dough and place in pastry tins, like a pie crust. Set remaining dough aside.

Filling (Chocolate):

1 c. milk
¼ c. cocoa
1 c. water
½ c. flour
1 c. sugar
1 tsp. Vanilla

Mix ingredients together and cook until thickened. Fill tins already lined with dough and cover each pasty with the remaining dough.

Brush the top of the pastry with a beaten egg yolk for shine.

Bake in 400° oven for 15 minutes.

Makes 12.

LEMON TORTE
....
Angela Frioni, Sr. Josita

1 c. flour
½ c. nuts
1 stick oleo

Mix flour, nuts, and oleo and place in a greased 9 x 13-inch pan. Bake at 350° for 15 minutes. Cool.

Filling:

8-oz. pkg. cream cheese
1 c. confectioners' sugar
1 c. Coolwhip

Soften the cream cheese, then add sugar. Fold in Cool Whip and spread on cooled crust.

Lemon Filling:
2 sm. pkgs. instant lemon pudding
2 ¾ c. milk

Mix together. When it starts to thicken, pour over above. Let set 1 hour, then top with remaining Cool Whip. Sprinkle with nuts. Refrigerate.

PASTRY TWISTS (CENCI ALIA FIORENTINA)
....
Amy Breton

1 c. plus 1 tsp. flour
Pinch of salt
Confectioners sugar
1 whole egg
1 egg yolk
2 tsp. rum
Oil for frying

Sift 1 cup of the flour, salt, and 1 teaspoon of confectioners sugar into a bowl. Make a well in the middle of the dough and add eggs and rum. Using the tips of your fingers, draw the flour in until the ingredients can be made into a ball.

Sprinkle the rest of the flour on a flat working surface and knead for 10 minutes until extra flour has been worked in and the dough is smooth and shiny. Wrap in foil and refrigerate for at least 1 hour.

Take half the dough and roll it out on the floured surface until paper thin. Cut into strips about ½ inch wide and 6 to 7 inches long. Tie into little knots and fry 4 to 5 at one time in deep hot oil until golden brown (about 1 to 2 minutes).

Repeat the above with the second batch of dough.

Before serving, sprinkle generously with confectioners sugar.

PIE CRUST

Phyllis DeMartini

1 lb. lard
1 tsp. baking soda
2 Tbsp. vinegar
8 oz. water
1 egg
5 c. flour
1 tsp. salt

Beat egg with a fork in 8 oz. measuring cup; add vinegar and fill with cold water to measuring cup 8 oz. mark. Cut lard and flour together with a pastry cutter. Add salt and soda. Mix together well. Chill overnight. Let stand 1/2 hour at room temperature before rolling out. The vinegar is the secret to the flaky crust.

ROSETTAS

Author Unknown

6 eggs
6 extra large spoons sugar
6 large spoon of oil
6 tsp vanilla
6 tsp black pepper
About 2 lbs. flour

Filling:
1 ½ c sugar
½ lb. walnuts
Cut fine cinnamon and cloves

Bake at 350° for 15 minutes.

ST. JOSEPH'S DAY CREAM PUFFS

Mickey Summa

Bring to boiling in saucepan:
1 c. hot water
½ c. butter
1 T. sugar
½ tsp. salt

Add, all at once:
1 c. sifted all-purpose flour

Lightly grease a cookie sheet. Beat vigorously with a wooden spoon until the mixture leaves the sides of the pan and forms a smooth ball (about 3 minutes). Remove from heat. Quickly beat in, one at a time, beating until smooth after each addition, 4 eggs. Continue beating until the mixture is smooth and glossy. Add, mixing thoroughly, 1 teaspoon grated orange peel and 1 teaspoon grated lemon peel. Drop by tablespoonfuls 2 inches apart on the baking sheet.

Bake at 350° for 15 minutes or until golden in color. Remove to rack to cool completely. Cut a slit inside of each puff and fill.

STRUFOLI / PIGNOLATA (FRIED)

Nina Hyde

4 to 5 c. flour
2 tsp. baking powder
1 tsp. salt
3 T. white wine
Colored sprinkles
¼ c. oil
6 eggs, beaten
1 (1½-lb.) jar honey
½ c. pine nuts
Oil for frying
Candied cherries, opt.

Mix flour, baking powder, and salt on a pastry board. Make a well, add wine, ¼ cup oil, and eggs, gradually blending ingredients with a fork. Mix to form a dough. Knead until smooth and soft. Cut dough in half. Roll each half into ¼ inch thickness.

Cut into ½-inch strips and roll each strip into a pencil shape. Cut pencil shape strips into ¼-inch pieces. Heat oil to 350°. Drop pieces into the oil (do not crowd). Stir to brown lightly. Remove to paper towels and cool.

Simmer honey to 350° on a candy thermometer or until a little honey drops into cold water, forms a soft ball. Remove from heat, stir in pine nuts, pour over strufoli, tossing to coat well. Top with sprinkles and candied cherries.

First Holy Communion, Gail Spadafora with grandmother Adeline and Aunt Emma Spadafora (1954)

PUDDING

GRANDMA DE SIMONE'S APPLE RICE PUDDING

Janine DeSimone Whilhelm

2¼ c. long-grain rice
Water
1 (32-oz.) bottle apple juice
½ c. sugar
Dash nutmeg, opt.
1 apple, peeled and cut into small pieces, opt.
¼ c. walnuts, opt.
Dash cinnamon

Cook rice in enough water to cover it for 5 minutes, then drain. Return to pan, add half of the bottle of apple juice, the apple and spices. Bring to boil and continue to add apple juice until cooked. Add nuts and sugar.

CUSTARD RICE PUDDING

Darlene Ferlo

6 eggs
¾ c. cooked rice
½ c. raisins
1 tsp. vanilla
¾ c. sugar
1 qt. skim milk

Beat eggs. Mix all ingredients together. Pour into a 10-inch glass baking dish. Top with cinnamon.

Bake at 375° for 20 minutes or until settled.

Fr. John Wood with Amy Benton and religious education class (c. 1986)

RICE PUDDING
....
Delcie Castro

1 c. washed rice
1 qt. milk
1 tsp. vanilla
½ c. sugar

Place all ingredients in a saucepan and allow it to come to a boil. Lower heat to lowest setting and stir until rice is cooked.

Pour into a bowl and sprinkle sugar and cinnamon on top.

May be served warm or cold.

MARSHMALLOW DELIGHT
....
A Friend

1 pkg. miniature marshmallows
2 small cans of Mandarin oranges
2 small cans of pineapple tidbits
¼ can of coconut bananas
3 small or 1 large sour cream

Mix all together and refrigerate overnight.

Fr. Nicholas Maio with Nina Daniello holding Louis Taverna

Add Your Own Recipes & Memories

Add Your Own Recipes & Memories

Add Your Own Recipes & Memories

Made in United States
North Haven, CT
09 December 2022

28304591R00115